A Tribe REBORN

HOW THE CLEVELAND INDIANS OF THE '90S WENT FROM CELLAR DWELLERS TO PLAYOFF CONTENDERS

GEORGE CHRISTIAN PAPPAS

FOREWORD BY HANK PETERS

SPORTS PUBLISHING

Sports Publishing books may be purchased in bulk at special discounts for sales promotion, corporate gifts, fund-raising, or educational purposes. Special editions can also be created to specifications. For details, contact the Special Sales Department, Sports Publishing, 307 West 36th Street, 11th Floor, New York, NY 10018 or sportspubbooks@skyhorsepublishing.com.

Sports Publishing® is a registered trademark of Skyhorse Publishing, Inc.®, a Delaware corporation.

Visit our website at www.sportspubbooks.com

10 9 8 7 6 5 4 3 2 1

Library of Congress Cataloging-in-Publication Data:
Pappas, George Christian.
  A tribe reborn : how the Cleveland Indians of the '90s went from cellar dwellers to playoff contenders / George Christian Pappas ; [foreword by] Henry J. Peters.
    pages cm.
  Summary: "A Tribe Reborn tells the story of a failing franchise, from "The Mistake by the Lake" to "The Curse of Rocky Colavito," and how a laughingstock team that was on the verge of relocating changed its ways to become a dominant franchise"--Provided by publisher.
  ISBN 978-1-61321-637-8 (hardback)
  1. Cleveland Indians (Baseball team)--History. I. Title.
  GV875.C7P36 2014
  796.357'640977132--dc23
                                        2013040401
Paperback ISBN: 978-1-68358-274-8
eBook ISBN: 978-1-68358-275-5

Cover design by Brian Peterson
Front cover photograph: AP Images

Printed in the United States of America

To my family: I would say something to the effect that you are my All-Stars, but you're so much more than that. I'm extraordinarily blessed to have you.

To the fans: 455 consecutive sellouts happened in Cleveland . . . first.

"It [Cleveland] is a sleeping giant. It only needs to be reawakened. That won't come with words, only action. But give fans what they want, a winning team, and they will react like no other city has."

—Gabe Paul, former Cleveland Indians executive, 1979

TABLE OF CONTENTS

PREFACE

$\mathbf{M}$y grandmother Irene was nine years old the last time the Indians won the World Series.

Back then, she rode the streetcar to Municipal Stadium on Lake Erie, accompanied by her older brother, Hipp, and sister, Helen. The Cleveland of her youth was a special place. After all, it had been the home of the nation's first traffic signal, the world's first city to be fully lighted by electricity, and the birthplace of Superman and Life Savers candies. Industrialist John D. Rockefeller made his fortune there and spent his final years living in one of the palatial estates on Millionaire's Row. Cleveland's Symphony Orchestra was included in America's elite "Big Five" classical ensembles, and its PlayhouseSquare Center was the nation's second largest theater complex after New York's Lincoln Center. Cleveland was indeed special, and so was its Tribe. But after the Tribe's last pennant in 1954, the city and its baseball team spiraled into four decades of decline. The Indians became perennial losers, the steel mills stopped producing, the city went bankrupt, and the mansions of Millionaire's Row started to vanish. (Rockefeller's manor was reduced to rubble to make room for a gas station and parking lot.)

Luckily for me, I was born in Cleveland just as the city and its baseball franchise were on the brink of their renaissance in the early nineties. I was treated to six divisional championships and two World Series appearances in the first eight years of Indians baseball that I can remember.

I learned to love the game of baseball from the left-field bleachers at Jacobs Field. It was a place where loud rock music pulsated over the loudspeakers, the aroma of hot dogs and Bertman original Ball Park Mustard drifted about the stadium concourse, and Slider, the Tribe's pink, fuzzy mascot, bounced around among the fans. Sellout crowds packed the place, and we all got to watch players like Albert Belle, Carlos Baerga, Eddie Murray, Sandy Alomar Jr., Jim Thome, and Manny Ramírez launch towering blasts into the seats. Omar Vizquel dazzled with his glove at shortstop and Kenny Lofton stole bases with ease. This was Indians baseball and as far as I knew, it had always been that way. Family members quickly point out that it wasn't.

Since this book was first published in 2014, the Cleveland sports scene has enjoyed another renaissance, highlighted by the Cavaliers' win over the Golden State Warriors in the NBA Finals and the Indians returning to the World Series in 2016. (Some joked that only a Cleveland team could allow the Chicago Cubs to end their 108-year championship drought.)

Watching the recent success from afar, I am reminded that the Cleveland of my youth was a special place. The Tribe of the nineties made me such a rabid baseball fan that I wore high socks and pointed my bat like Thome—a 2018 Hall of Fame inductee—throughout my Little League days. They say your past has a hand in shaping your future. Through those experiences, I knew I wanted to spend my life around the diamond. Today, I work in the player development department of a major-league club, heavily influenced by the players, coaches, and Indians personnel who made me a fan in the first place.

FOREWORD

The history of the Indians is a mixture of success and failure. While the game as it is played on the field has changed very little over the years, how to run a club and be successful is constantly changing. The ownership of the Indians went through many changes from the mid-fifties until the Jacobs brothers bought the club prior to the 1987 season. The one thing that remained constant through all the changes was losing. That first year of ownership was not a successful nor happy one for the new owners. The losing continued, and they knew something had to be done or baseball would be dead in Cleveland.

When Dick Jacobs called me in late October of 1987 after my twelve-year run as general manager of the Baltimore Orioles had ended, he mentioned how he'd like to talk about me possibly running the Indians. My first reaction was: *Do I really want to do this?* In order to understand my hesitation, you need to know two things:

1. I had spent six rather miserable years with the Indians from 1966 through 1971;
2. From what I knew about the current Indians, the organization was in bad shape, beginning with the playing personnel and extending to the front office and player-development program.

The task ahead was not one of rebuilding, but one of starting over from scratch.

The state of the Indians reminded me of my experiences with the Kansas City Athletics when I took a job there as farm and scouting director in January of 1955, after Connie Mack sold the Philadelphia A's and the club had moved to Kansas City. At the time of the move, the club had one scout; no major-league prospects among the 96 players on the roster of four minor-league clubs that had no managers; and, finally, a last-place major-league club.

I would like to claim that I enjoyed immediate success in building the player development and scouting staff, but that was not the case. Funding needed to accomplish the task was limited. Progress in the early years was slow, except in building a scouting staff. We came up with a couple of future stars like Clete Boyer and Ken Harrelson, but not too many others.

When Charlie Finley bought the A's in 1961, he was willing to provide the funding needed to make things happen. It was during this period from 1961–1965, when a solid scouting staff was in place, that the majority of the players who eventually became World Champions, after the A's moved to Oakland, were signed and developed by the organization. This group included current Hall of Fame players Catfish Hunter, Rollie Fingers, and Reggie Jackson. While it took years to build a winner, progress can come quickly once you have developed a solid staff of talented, dedicated people; coupled with the funding required.

When I decided to resign as general manager of the A's after the 1965 season, my good friend Gabe Paul, then the general manager of the Indians, offered me the job of farm club and scouting director. I left Kansas City with great regret, as I knew the organization was loaded with talent, but I'd had enough of Charlie Finley and chose not to work for him any longer.

Joining the Indians then was not unlike joining the A's in '55. The major-league club was better than the A's, but the player development program was weak: a small scouting staff, small farm system, and very few prospects among their minor-league players. And last but not least, no funds were available for improvement.

I did a study my second year with the club to determine why the team had slipped so badly since the mid-fifties. The results of the study did not shock me. It was primarily due to a failure to produce major-league players. They had a few now and then, but not in sufficient numbers to produce a winner. During my time there, we produced a few good ones like Buddy Bell, Chris Chambliss, Ray Fosse, Dick Tidrow, John Lowenstein, and Mike Paul, but again, not enough to create a winner.

If I thought the job of building a winner was all but hopeless, I was convinced of it following the 1970 season. Vernon Stouffer, a very likeable man and then owner of the club, told me following a Board of Directors meeting that the 1971 budget for player development and scouting was being cut by 50 percent. He then asked me how badly the cuts would hurt us. I responded by telling him that if he intended to sell the club within the next couple of years, it would not hurt too much. However, if he was in it for the long haul, then the club just committed suicide. The rest is history. Stouffer sold the club within two years. The losing and suffering that started in the mid-fifties continued through the sixties, seventies, and eighties.

* * *

Please do not think this is a foreword about Hank Peters. I have related my experiences with the Kansas City A's and Cleveland Indians from 1966–1971 so you will have some understanding of why some clubs win and some lose, and most importantly, what a club needs if it expects to produce a winning team.

When Dick Jacobs bought the Indians, he didn't get much for his buck. He was, however, a smart and successful business man who knew very little about running a baseball club. He recognized that he had to bring in some experienced baseball people with successful backgrounds in order to develop a winning team, both on and off the field.

When we first met to discuss my joining the Indians as President and General Manager, I told him much of what I have related to you thus far in this foreword. I also told him of the success we enjoyed during my years with the Orioles, why we had been successful, and what it took to sign and develop Hall of Fame players Brooks Robinson, Jim Palmer, Eddie Murray, and Cal Ripken Jr.

I explained that I knew no shortcuts to develop a winning team. Trades, if successful, could help; free agent signings at the proper time might help; but you had to start with the basics and the people you hire. A club will never become a winner until it starts to produce its own talent. Producing talent requires good scouting, successful free-agent drafts of amateur players, and a solid player-development program. All of that requires funding that owner-ship must provide if the club is unable to generate sufficient income to fund its needs. Playing games at the lakefront stadium under a lease agreement that provided very little financial benefits for the club virtually assured any owner of the Indians that he would be the one who would be providing the funds.

I was sixty-three years old when Dick approached me, and had forty-one years of baseball experience. I told him if I took the job, it would be for only four years. And then I gave him the bad news—we would not be a winner during those four years.

I then explained that I would try to create the framework for a winner by bringing in talented and dedicated people to staff the front office and player-development programs, and we would start adding players capable of playing on a winning team. Some would come from our own player-development program (Jim Thome, Manny Ramírez, Albert Belle, Charles Nagy) and others would come from trades (Sandy Alomar Jr., Carlos Baerga, Kenny Lofton).

Dick said he and his brother were in this for the long haul, and would provide the funds required. He also assured me of a free hand in doing whatever I thought I needed to do to get results. With that assurance and commitment, I agreed to come aboard.

A lot of changes took place during my four years at the helm. A team of front office staff members was assembled, including but not limited to: Tom Giordano, John Hart, Dan O'Dowd, Dennis Lehman, Bob DiBiasio, Jeff Overton, Mike Seghi, and Ken Stefanov. Many are still with the Indians after these many years. The baseball department prospered and put the finishing touches to the pennant-winning teams that made the Indians a success on and off the field. Some are still enjoying success as baseball executives.

Is there a lesson in all this? You bet there is. If you are a club that is down and out, find yourself a Dick Jacobs!

Enjoy the book.

—Hank Peters

Introduction

A TICKER TAPE PARADE OF SORTS

October 30, 1995

They were rocking in the streets of Cleveland.

The city had waited more than forty-one years for a celebration following the 1954 World Series. That much time had passed since Cleveland had a winning team.[1] Heck, most fans had not yet been born or were too young to remember the last time the Indians had even competed in the postseason. In that span, they'd gone from being hapless to almost a little hopeless, with rumors surfacing each year like trash in the Cuyahoga River that their beloved Tribe was on their way out of town.[2] The losing had become so commonly accepted across America that even Hollywood parodied the ball club and its dubious roster full of nobodies *actually winning* (a hilarious concept, right?) in the successful 1989 comedy *Major League*. But this time the winning was

---

[1] It had been nine years since the Indians had a winning record (1986; 84–78), and the team only had ten winning seasons (1955–56, 58–59, '65, '68, '76, '79, '81, and '86) in forty years (1955–94). During that span, they had a .477 winning percentage.

[2] Talk began as early as the 1960s that the Indians would relocate due to poor attendance and changes in ownership. This will be discussed further in the chapters that follow.

1

real, and nothing—not even the potential of sleet and snow in the forecast—would keep them from celebrating on that Monday in October.

For all intents and purposes, the city shut down for a day of revelry. Loudspeakers bumped Jock Jams hits like "Get Ready for This" and "Rock and Roll Part 2." Men and women skipped work and pulled their kids out of school. The mayor and his delegation from City Hall waved flags from the back of a flatbed adorned with red, white, and blue balloons. Cheerleaders chirped and high school bands marched, the flared-out bells of their sousaphones (a brass instrument) inscribed with players' last names and jersey numbers. Even the ECTO-1, the Ghostbusters' converted hearse, flew a flag bearing the grinning likeness of Chief Wahoo up the parade route. The Indians had crossed their own streams, and for one day, the team's spectres had been zapped, trapped, and locked away.

The celebration continued toward Public Square—a ten-acre plaza in the center of the city—around which its tallest buildings, the Old Stone Church, and the former Higbee's department store were built. Main roads into the downtown area converge upon the Square. In the Square is a statue of Moses Cleaveland, the city's founder, who envisioned the space serving as a village green and a primary civic meeting place in its early days.[3] In keeping with the tradition, Cleveland's annual parades and major celebrations end up at the Square.

Some 50,000 overjoyed fans showed up there two Fridays earlier, on the eve of the World Series, to express their devotion to the Tribe at a citywide rally. Bob Feller was among them. The Hall of Fame right-hander had won 19 games in 1948, pitching the Indians to their first world championship since 1920. He also helped them to their last playoff appearance (and last league pennant) in 1954.

"This is just like 1948, only bigger," he told reporters at the event.

The modern fanfare might have made it appear that way to Feller, but in all, 200,000 "friends of the Feathered" lined the way from Euclid Avenue to Public Square after *his* team won the Series. However, Feller, who at this point was seventy-six years old, had watched the Indians endure more than forty

---

[3] Recreational baseball games had also been played in the Square since the 1840s.

depressing seasons without reaching the playoffs. Because of this, he would certainly not be holding back his excitement or optimism.

"We had the best ball club in America then and we've got the best ball club in America now," Feller said, comparing the two.

The 1948 Indians produced six Hall of Famers. They had five All-Stars,, three of whom started in the Midsummer Classic for the American League. Gene Bearden was the AL ERA champ in his rookie campaign, Bob Lemon was the *Sporting News* Pitcher of the Year, and Lou Boudreau, the player-manager (they still had those back then), finished second to Ted Williams for the batting title, but was named Most Valuable Player by the season's end.[4]

Compared to the champs of '48, how did the '95 Indians stack up? *They* had seven .300 hitters in the lineup—three of whom would reach the elite 500 home run club—and one man who had just clubbed his 3,000th career hit earlier in the year. There were six All-Stars, three of whom started the game for the AL. They had an unflappable closer, who nailed down an Indian-record 46 saves in 48 opportunities. Their shortstop won his third of nine consecutive Gold Glove awards, and was well on his way toward establishing himself as the best defensive player at that position of the decade, if not baseball history.

But after the Series, each of these two great Tribe teams could claim what the other could not. On one hand, the Indians of '95 had thumped their chests at opponents, pounded on their teammates' helmets after dramatic, come-from-behind victories, and won over the hearts of two generations of Cleveland baseball fans who hadn't known a winning Indians team since 1948. On the other, Feller's team actually paraded into town as world champions.

See, the Indians lost the 1995 World Series to the Atlanta Braves in six games.

The fans in Cleveland partied anyway.

An outsider reading this might find it to be rather paradoxical, but where else would you find a parade to celebrate a losing team? The North

---

[4] Boudreau was also the first shortstop to ever win the award.

Side of Chicago, where the Cubs hadn't won in forever? Buffalo, where the Bills dropped four consecutive Super Bowls? This could only happen in Cleveland, where the sun shines just sixty-six days a year, the River used to catch on fire, and the last championship franchise among the four major sports was crowned before the Super Bowl even existed.[5] This is not to say that the Cleveland sports scene was completely a lost cause: The Browns and Cavaliers saw periods of promise, but just when the fans saw a shimmer of hope, fate reared its ugly head and gave them reruns of heartbreak:

Red Right 88. The Drive. The Fumble. Jordan over Ehlo. And so on . . .

Although the Indians had won the American League pennant (their first since 1954), the players felt like their '95 season was just the next installment of the city's misfortune. They had just been on the brink of ending the title drought, and now they had to return to Cleveland having let down the fans.

"I couldn't believe the season was over," said Carlos Baerga, the Tribe's second baseman, who flew out to end the Series. "Every game in the regular season and the playoffs, every time we were coming back and winning. . . . We thought it was going to be the same, but it didn't happen. When you have that kind of confidence, it's like hitting a wall. I said, 'Oh, my God! What just happened?! We want to keep playing!' But that's when it was all over."

So imagine the surprise when Baerga and his teammates arrived to find the entire city waiting to celebrate with them.

"It was special to come home and see our fans cheering for us," added Baerga.

But to the chagrin of the fans, the players didn't participate in the city's parade; they wanted to save that special tradition for the future, after bringing that elusive championship back to Cleveland. Instead, the team bused from the stadium to the Square in time for a special ceremony, during which they

---

[5] The 1964 Cleveland Browns won the NFL Championship Game against the Baltimore Colts, 27–0.

could personally thank all of their supporters. Players, coaches, and team personnel came off their Lakefront Lines charters one by one, making their way along the red carpet to the stage set up in front of Terminal Tower.

Indians manager Mike Hargrove led the way, stopping periodically to smile and wave. Along with him came the team's general manager, John Hart. The players shuffled off the bus and strutted like rock stars before a show, some wearing jeans and long overcoats. Utility infielder Álvaro Espinoza sported a suede jacket and a black cowboy hat, platoon outfielder Wayne Kirby a leather bomber and dark, rounded sunglasses. Kenny Lofton, the Indians' center fielder and self-declared best dresser, got on the microphone to tease Baerga for being the only one in a suit. (Baerga was especially festive in his red blazer, which he wore over a fitted black t-shirt and gold chain.) The act continued with shortstop Omar Vizquel joking about having been mistaken for Braves second baseman Mark Lemke at an Atlanta shopping mall during the World Series. The crowd couldn't get enough of it, erupting with laughter and applause after each remark.

The fans couldn't have dreamt this four years earlier, when Cleveland had lost more than 100 games and finished last in the league standings and fan attendance. In the span of only a few years, the franchise had somehow managed to pull off a complete 180-degree reversal. Now the Indians were winners of 100 games—the best record in the league—and would eventually sell out the entire upcoming season before Opening Day. They were no longer the loveable lakefront losers. The proof was on display in Public Square, with the players performing standup comedy routines and promising them a champion. "Don't be surprised if that happens next year," Lofton said.

How in the name of Moses Cleaveland had it come to this?

Chapter One

"MISTAKES" ON THE LAKE

A precursor to the Indians' prolonged decline and eventual revival was an ironic publicity stunt in 1949; one that seemed totally harmless at the time, but nonetheless, would come to haunt the ball club for years. The stunt came the year after Cleveland had won the World Series. Bill Veeck, the Tribe's owner since 1946, was already known around baseball as a maverick showman for his eye-catching and oft-ridiculous antics, which brought enough fans into the ballpark to set a new major-league attendance record in '48. Sometimes his actions created controversy, like when he installed movable fences in the outfield to benefit Indians pitchers. (The American League later passed a rule outlawing that practice.) Some of his actions were historically significant, like when he helped integrate the American League with the signing of Negro League star Larry Doby, or when he moved the Indians out of League Park and into Municipal Stadium for good.[1] Most of his actions were quite

---

[1] The Indians had played home games in League Park since 1901 (their first season in the AL), but in the 1930s began splitting their schedule between that and the larger Cleveland Municipal Stadium.

gimmicky, like the time he hired Max Patkin, the "Clown Prince of Baseball," to masquerade on the field as a coach. But none of Veeck's tricks was more ridiculous than the one he pulled after his Indians had been mathematically eliminated from contention in 1949.

When it was clear that the Tribe would not repeat as champions, he staged a funeral at Municipal Stadium to bury their title hopes—and the '48 pennant flag.

The supposedly solemn ceremony took place on Friday, September 23, minutes before Cleveland was scheduled to play Detroit. Veeck officiated the burial, dressed in black and wearing a top hat. He ordered the '48 pennant flag to be lowered from its post high above center field, where it had flown proudly all season long. He placed it in the back of a horse-drawn hearse and led it in a procession along the warning track, starting in right field near the bullpen. Indians players joined the procession from the home dugout, with team officials acting as pallbearers. The fans were instructed to mourn the passing of the pennant, which was buried in a coffin beyond the center-field wall about 410 feet from home plate and then forgotten.[2]

Veeck's act looked like nothing more than another one of his quirky promotions in the seasons that immediately followed, as the Indians remained a competitive team, kept afloat by aging All-Stars and new faces. They finished second to the New York Yankees in the AL each year from 1951 to 1953, then won a major-league best 111 games in 1954 to take the pennant in the Junior Circuit and secure a spot in the World Series for the second time in six years. However, this time around, the Fall Classic didn't end as well as it did in '48. Willie Mays made his now-famous over-the-shoulder catch and spinning throw from the warning track of the Polo Grounds in the first game, and the New York Giants went on to sweep the Series. Cleveland's record

---

[2] The championship pennant's whereabouts remain unknown even today.

began to decline shortly thereafter, dipping below the .500 threshold in 1957 for the first time in eleven years.[3]

Poor attendance and sixth-place finish had the Indians looking for a replacement general manager who would generate Veeckian interest around the club, and they selected Frank Lane as their fix.

Frank Lane had been nicknamed "Trader" Lane long before he took over in Cleveland. He was a sensationalist and frequently dealt players to keep his teams in the papers. Case in point: Lane executed 241 trades over seven years as the general manager of the Chicago White Sox. He knew transactions involving more reputable players caused an even greater commotion. After his hire by the Cardinals in October of 1955, Lane tried sending St. Louis hero Stan Musial to the Philadelphia Phillies in exchange for star pitcher Robin Roberts. Team owner August Busch stopped that deal after talk of the proposed swap aired over the radio.[4]

Unlike Busch, Cleveland's ownership didn't intervene when Lane made a blockbuster trade just three weeks after being introduced. He started dealing on December 4, 1957, when he sent Al Smith and Early Wynn to the White Sox for Minnie Miñoso and Fred Hatfield. Wynn joined the Indians in 1949 and became part of their "Big Four" rotation with Bob Feller, Bob Lemon, and Mike Garcia. He won 20 or more games four times (1951, '52, '54, and '56)

---

[3] The 1957 Indians finished the season with a 76–77 record.

[4] Stan Musial was elected to the National Baseball Hall of Fame in 1969. As of 2013, Musial is still the Cardinals all-time leader in games played (3,026), at-bats (10,972), plate appearances (12,717), runs scored (1,949), hits (3,630), total bases (6,134), singles (2,253), doubles (725), triples (177), home runs (475), RBI (1,951), and walks (1,599).

Robin Roberts was elected to the National Baseball Hall of Fame in 1976. As of 2013, Roberts is still the Phillies all-time leader in games played (529), innings pitched (3,739.1), complete games (272), and is second in wins (234), strikeouts (1,871), and games started (472).

Both players have their numbers retired.

before being dealt. Lane later traded Miñoso and three others back to Chicago on December 6, 1959, for Norm Cash, Bubba Phillips, and John Romano.[5] The trade would have worked out fine if Lane hadn't turned around and sent Cash to Detroit four months later for Steve Demeter. Cash never played a game for the Indians, but went on to hit 355 career home runs over the next fifteen years as the Tigers' everyday first baseman.

Of course, by then, Rocky Colavito was more than just a sensation in Cleveland; "The Rock," as he was known, had become a cult icon. He was a charismatic, handsome figure to whom fans gravitated. Rocky accommodated their autograph requests and clobbered home runs, once smacking four homers in consecutive at-bats in Baltimore's vast Memorial Stadium. He was one of the dominant power hitters in the AL; hitting 41 homers in '58 (one short of Mickey Mantle's league lead) and another 42 in 1959, sharing the home-run crown with the Washington Senators' third baseman, Harmon Killebrew. That's why fans and writers alike didn't quite understand why Lane would consider trading him in the first place.

If there were any harbingers for a curse associated with the Indians' eventual trade of Rocky Colavito, look no further than Roger Maris for evidence. Lane had originally tried sending Colavito to the Kansas City Athletics for a package of seven players in 1958, but the A's thought his asking price was too steep, and so the two teams settled on another deal: Cleveland sent second-year player Roger Maris, Preston Ward, and Dick Tomanek to Kansas City for Woodie Held and Vic Power. Three years later, Maris broke Babe Ruth's single-season home-run record, helped the Yankees to their nineteenth and twentieth world championships, and would appropriately be named the Most Valuable Player in the AL in 1960 and '61.

Lane again found a way to make headlines, trading Colavito before the Indians opened the 1960 season. The Detroit Tigers were coming to Cleveland, and what better a way to send shockwaves around baseball than by trading the Rock to the visiting club for Harvey Kuenn, the reigning batting

---

[5] The trade also included Dick Brown, Don Ferrarese, and Jake Striker.

champion. Indians fans exploded with anger, and showed it by boycotting games.[6] It also didn't help that Lane was quoted, after the trade, as saying "What's all the fuss about? All I did was trade hamburger for steak." But they didn't come to call it the "Curse of Rocky Colavito" overnight.

The trade itself was a giant flop. Lane's successor, Gabe Paul, later told *Cleveland Plain Dealer* columnist Terry Pluto, "The Indians traded a slow guy with power for a slow guy with no power." And Paul was right. Kuenn went on to compile only 87 home runs in his fifteen-year career.[7] He spent one season in Cleveland before being again traded, this time to the Giants for Johnny Antonelli and Willie Kirkland. Colavito, in turn, went on to add another 251 homers to his career stat-line after the trade.

After the obvious hiccup, Lane tried to right his wrong. His quick fix: attempting to trade entire rosters with the Chicago White Sox. When the Commissioner's office shot down his attempt, he became the first executive in baseball history to trade managers, dispatching Joe Gordon to Detroit, of all places, for Tigers skipper Jimmy Dykes. But by that point, it was too late; and the Indians' record plummeted under water twenty-eight times over the next thirty-four years. Looking for a scapegoat, some fans suggested Colavito's trade cursed the franchise and brought about three decades of futility. Pluto even wrote a book, *The Curse of Rocky Colavito*, to chronicle the Indians' slump. Colavito insisted he didn't conjure any such curse, but the Indians, at times, seemed to be cursed by their own doing.

For example, Gabe Paul tried reversing the spell in 1965, but his plan failed miserably. He gave up pitching prospect Tommy John and outfielder Tommie Agee to bring back the fan favorite, Colavito, who was then thirty-two years old and in his eleventh season. The result? John, who had only two wins under his belt as a rookie, went on to register an additional 286 in his twenty-six-year career. Agee was the Rookie of the Year and featured prominently in center field when the "Miracle" New York Mets won the 1969

---

[6] Attendance in 1960 fell by almost 500,000 from the previous year.

[7] Kuenn hit 9 home runs in the 1960 season for Cleveland.

World Series. Colavito went on to play just three more seasons before retiring to a mushroom farm outside of Reading, Pennsylvania. And just like that, the Curse of Rocky Colavito seemed like a real thing. Among other mishaps, Cleveland fans had plenty to blame the curse for:

Ray Fosse, catcher

Fosse suffered a separated shoulder in the 1970 All-Star Game after Pete Rose collided with him at home plate. The injury sidetracked the potential star, who was plagued with injuries for the rest of his career.

Wayne Garland, pitcher

Garland injured his arm in his first spring training appearance with the Indians. Garland was a twenty-game winner for the Orioles in 1976, and had just signed a ten-year contract with Cleveland. Garland opted to pitch through pain after the injury instead of undergoing surgery, and posted a 28–48 record over the next five seasons and retired at age thirty.

Dennis Eckersley, pitcher

The trade of twenty-three-year-old Dennis Eckersley to Boston in March of 1978 on paper seems quite questionable. However, this trade was necessary, after Eckersley's wife fell in love with his best friend and teammate, Rick Manning. "Eck" enjoyed back-to-back seasons with twenty wins for the Red Sox and eventually became a Hall of Fame closer, saving 390 games over his career.

Joe Charboneau, outfielder, designated hitter

The Baseball Gods giveth, and the Baseball Gods taketh away. "Super Joe" became the first player to be named Rookie of the Year (1980, .289 BA, 131 H, 23 HR, 87 RBI) and then wind up back in the minors the next season (.247 BA, 29 H, 4 HR, 18 RBI), where he hit a meager .217 clip for Triple-A Charleston after being demoted 48 games into his sophomore campaign. He would only play 22 games more in his career, and was out of baseball at the age of twenty-six.

On the field, the Indians had become a laughingstock. Off the field, the franchise was riddled with problems. Since Veeck sold the club, ownership had changed hands nine times, with each principal leaving behind debts for his successor. It took until 1986 for the right influential Clevelander to decide that he had seen enough and to take an interest in buying the team. That man was Dick Jacobs.

Chapter Two

JACOBS' PURCHASE

People who knew Richard E. "Dick" Jacobs often said he was so modest, they would not have known the man had even a quarter to his name; but anyone could have dispelled any such notion by just looking at him. He was a tall man (6-foot-3 to be exact) with white hair and an expensive taste in clothing that harkened back to the 1950s mode. Once he acquired the Indians, his dress shirts had French cuffs added and he started wearing custom-made gold links with an etching of Chief Wahoo.

By then, Dick was sixty-one and a bachelor, three years removed from a divorce, which allowed him the freedom to come and go as he pleased between Cleveland and his second-favorite city, New York, on either of his two private planes. The trip had become routine for him during those days. He was finishing a $5-million renovation of his swanky four-story townhouse in Manhattan and jetted to the Big Apple once a week to inspect the project. The 120-year-old residence also doubled as a second office, and he outfitted it with antique furnishings, sculptures, and artwork to give it an eighteenth-century London feel. Oil paintings by Old Masters and nineteenth-century European watercolors hung from the walls like the wings of galleries on the

Upper East Side. In Cleveland, Jacobs lived in a two-floor penthouse suite that offered far-reaching scenic views of Lake Erie. When he was in town, he preferred to ride around comfortably in his enormous 1976 Cadillac and a four-door Lincoln, which he had customized into a convertible. If he was in the mood for a leisurely getaway, he also had a fourteen-room ranch an hour from downtown Los Angeles, dubbed "The Chateau," which sat on 25 acres in Hidden Valley, California. He shared the villa with his brother, David, and their business partner, Dominic Visconsi. To say that Dick liked to enjoy a lavish lifestyle wherever he went is indeed an understatement.

But Dick didn't always have those conveniences, and he never seemed to forget that for as long as he lived. During his youth, he could smell the rubber burning inside the tire plant where his father worked from the front yard of their home in Akron's Goodyear Heights. He earned his first nickels and dimes mowing lawns as a ten-year-old during the Great Depression, and got his first job peeling potatoes for french fries at Swensons, the area's famed drive-in burger joint. Dick ascended in the ranks after a year in the kitchen and became a carhop (waiter/waitress at a drive-in restaurant). That's when he began cultivating a shrewd sense for business. He could spot a Cadillac coming from two blocks away and would claim it before the other carhops could, knowing that waiting on the nicer cars guaranteed the best tips. That same carhop made it into *Forbes Magazine* in 1986 with an estimated worth of $500 million. Dick had quietly become one of the wealthiest developers in the world, let alone Cleveland. He was the chairman and CEO of Jacobs, Visconsi, Jacobs & Company, whose assets included twenty-five Wendy's hamburger franchises in metropolitan New York, about forty shopping malls in sixteen states, forty townhouses in Ft. Lauderdale, the popular Pier House Resort on Duval Street in Key West, and a partnership with Marriott Hotels. His group had also just sold a chain of fifty greeting-card stores to Cleveland-based American Greetings when Dick decided to make another investment and add a Major League Baseball franchise to his accumulation of lucrative ventures.

There is irony in the fact that the Jacobs brothers formed the contracting company responsible for their fortune in 1954; the last time the Indians won the AL pennant. The brothers were avid Cleveland sports fans, having witnessed the Tribe's glory days of the forties and fifties, as well as the team's spiraling free-fall from grace. David Jacobs and his wife, Barbara, enjoyed the company of another Greater Cleveland-native, New York Yankees owner George Steinbrenner, at occasional dinners and social gatherings.[1]

The brothers were looking for a new opportunity and approached the Indians in 1986, when the franchise didn't have a living owner.[2]

Three years had passed since the last owner, Francis J. "Steve" O'Neill, died in August of 1983. He was a lifelong Cleveland resident whose family made a mint in the trucking industry. O'Neill purchased a minority interest in the team in 1961 and sold his stake in 1973 to partner with Steinbrenner's group that bought the Yankees, but cashed out on his share of the Bronx Bombers after five years to buy back a principal interest in the Tribe. His nephew, Pat O'Neill, was put in charge of the sale of the club after his death and feared that a new owner might cart the franchise out of the city they had called home since 1894. That could have been a very real possibility without someone who could invest in a new park for the floundering club.

* * *

There had been overtures to try and lure the team away from Cleveland in years past. One plan during William R. Daley's ownership had the Indians moving to Seattle by 1970. Vernon Stouffer bought into the franchise in 1964, stopping that move from ever taking place. But Stouffer later had a $2.5 million agreement with investors in New Orleans to have the Indians play thirty games of their home schedule at the Superdome. Dallas and

---

[1] Steinbrenner hailed from nearby Rocky River, a suburb situated about ten miles west of the downtown Cleveland area.

[2] Francis J. "Steve" O'Neill owned the Indians from 1978 until his death in 1983. From 1983–86, the organization was run by O'Neill's estate, until the Jacobs brothers stepped in.

Oakland also made presentations before the team owners at different times, with Houston and Minnesota being rumored as potential destinations as well. All the while, the *Plain Dealer* ran stories with photos of every partner from the club's ownership group on the top of the sports section, blasting them as the men to blame if the Indians were ever to leave town. But thankfully, those plans never took shape. As attendance numbers continued to decline, Cleveland trickled into the group of clubs rumored to be on the move in the era of expansion. At that time, the Oakland A's talk of relocation southward to Fremont or San Jose was almost subverted by the possibility of playing in the Superdome. The Pirates nearly headed westward to Denver in 1985. That same year, Cleveland only managed to draw a little more than 655,000 fans to Municipal Stadium, finishing with the league's worst fan attendance for a third consecutive season. St. Petersburg, Florida, was named as a possible destination for relocation, as the city had been trying to draw the White Sox, Mariners, and Giants. Pat O'Neill didn't want to see the Indians go there, either. He decided that only another Clevelander would make the team's stay possible, and Dick Jacobs had a genuine sense about him from the moment he came to inquire about purchasing the franchise.

"Is this team for sale? No messing around," he asked.

It was a legitimate question. There had been some talk that O'Neill might hold onto the franchise. He hadn't sold it in the more than two years that he'd been owner, and they were only accumulating more debt the longer he kept them. But the Indians' performance in 1986 sparked an increase in demand for suitors that he couldn't ignore. The team drew almost 1.5 million fans for its highest attendance figure since 1959 (the year before the Colavito trade), and under the direction of team president Peter Bavasi, the Indians turned a paltry $100,000 profit, the first black ink in three decades. With that in mind, O'Neill decided to listen to Jacobs.

"Cleveland's on the upswing," Jacobs professed, "and we want to be a part of it."

He wasn't kidding around. The Jacobs brothers had big plans to revive the city. They had just spent $43 million to buy and redevelop the 40-floor

Erieview Tower. They would soon be opening the Galleria; a glass-enclosed shopping center adjacent to it on East 9th Street. It would be the first retail mall the downtown area had ever seen. Two years later, they would break ground on the 57-story Society Center (known later as the Key Tower), the tallest building in the United States between New York and Chicago.

Even Dick's thirty-three-year-old son, Jeff, a former Republican state representative, had a finger in urban development, independent of his father's influence. Jeff was overseeing the creation of Nautica, a mixed-use water-front project with a bar, restaurant, and boardwalk that would help invigorate nightlife in the bustling Flats area along the Cuyahoga River.

Given the Jacobs family's influence at City Hall, Dick also promised to lobby for a new stadium of its own. The Indians weren't making any money as the Browns' tenants at Municipal Stadium, and couldn't support themselves drawing 2,000 to 3,000 fans a night.

The estate of F. J. "Steve" O'Neill heard interest from at least five more local parties who offered more money to buy the team, but Pat cast aside those other bids. He believed in the Jacobs brothers' commitment to civic-mindedness and sports wrapped into one. If he were to find a bene-factor out in northeast Ohio to revitalize the Indians, it was going to be Dick Jacobs.

Pat O'Neill told the Jacobs brothers that they would have forty-five days, starting July 1, to confirm their decision to buy the club and all of its assets for $35.5 million, plus another $12 million to cover the team's debts. The actual breakdown of the purchase ended up totaling $18 million in cash, $3 million from a loan to the O'Neill estate, and another $14 million to settle outstanding bank loans from previous owners. The sum was pocket change for Dick Jacobs.

Owners of other major-league teams were surprised that such an accomplished businessman wanted to make a sizeable investment in Cleveland base-ball, but they were also very pleased. There was unanimous support among the owners for the Jacobs brothers' bid, which, as former commissioner Peter Ueberroth noted, was a rarity.

"[Dick] cares dearly about his community and did not want the team to leave," Ueberroth said in a 1987 interview for *Cleveland Magazine*. "We see him as a no-nonsense guy, and baseball needs that."

Accordingly, the American League approved the sale December 11, 1986, recognizing Dick Jacobs as the principal owner and David as his partner.

Chapter Three

HANK PETERS AND THE BASEBALL MEN

The sale of the Cleveland Indians to Dick and David Jacobs in 1986 coincided with rising expectations surrounding the ball club. The team had just completed its first winning season since the players went on strike in 1981, posting an 84–78 record, its best since 1968 (when they went 86–75). The Indians finished six games behind the rival Yankees and 11 and a half games out of a playoff spot, which led the media to tab Cleveland as the dark-horse candidate to win the American League East in 1987; the brothers' inaugural season. Sluggers Cory Snyder and Joe Carter appeared on the cover of the April 6 issue of *Sports Illustrated* under the headline "Indian Uprising." The magazine touted the Tribe as the best squad in the league.

SI columnist Ron Fimrite wrote: "Believe it or not, something is happening in Cleveland. Cleveland?" he prodded, "You mean the river's on fire again? It stopped snowing? You got a new joke? C'mon, what do you mean? The football season's been over for almost three months."

But Fimrite continued, boldly declaring: "It's like 1948 all over again. There's a feeling that this is the year."

While the media buzzed, the truth was that the Jacobs brothers had no background running a Major League Baseball franchise, and their new undertaking threw them their first curveball long before Opening Day. Peter Bavasi, who had been the Indians' president at the time of the sale, left his post one month after the brothers took over. Dick and David decided not to replace him immediately, choosing first to observe; to learn more about their new business and understand its inner-workings before bringing anyone else on board. The entrepreneurial strategy they found to be most critical to managing a successful operation with their previous ventures was to entrust the staff with carrying out its responsibilities. As principal owner of the Indians, that meant Dick Jacobs would refrain from putting his hands into making baseball decisions. He would instead leave that task to his franchise's baseball men. Of those he inherited after Bavasi's departure, Dan O'Brien and Joe Klein were in charge.

Dan O'Brien had more than thirty years of service in the major and minor leagues before arriving in Cleveland to work under Bavasi as the assistant to the president. The Indians' past ownership hired O'Brien after he served as president and, later, general manager of the Seattle Mariners, though they never broke .500 during his tenure.[1] His prior major-league experience also included five years as the GM of the Texas Rangers, who were competitive but never enough to win the American League West crown. O'Brien had also spent ten years as the assistant to the president of the National Association of Professional Baseball (essentially the governing body for the minor leagues), the latter half of which he was a top aide to Hank Peters (his name will appear again soon).

Joe Klein had come up as a first baseman in the Washington Senators organization in the 1960s before managing their minor-league clubs. He continued managing after the Senators became the Rangers in 1972, and then transitioned into the front office, where he served as the director of

---

[1] O'Brien worked for the Mariners from 1978–83, and the team's combined record while he was president ('79–83) and general manager ('81–83) was 306–451 (.404).

scouting and player development before ultimately being promoted to GM in 1982. He was let go after three losing seasons, and spent one year as the assistant GM for John Schuerholz and the 1985 World Series-winning Kansas City Royals. The Indians brought him on the following year as GM and vice president of baseball operations, and they improved enough to have been thought of as possible contenders out of the gate in preseason.

But as fate would have it, 1987 was not the Indians' year at all. Writers clarified that point—Fimrite himself owned up to it on behalf of *Sports Illustrated* in his column in late June, when the Indians were already "a million games behind, completely out of the running."

He addressed his prediction: "Prognosticators—like *SI's*—who said Cleveland would be the best team in the American League were maybe a tad off."

The Indians went on to lose 101 games and finished the season with the league's worst record, as if cursed by the magazine's alleged cover jinx. Dick Jacobs was concerned that his investment would continue to falter, and soon realized that he couldn't take the team to the next level without the right leadership in the front office. Thus, the search began around baseball for some executive leadership.

Around the same time in Baltimore, the Orioles were about to give their front office a major facelift. Owner Edward Bennett Williams fired his executive president and general manager, Henry J. "Hank" Peters, the day after the regular season ended.

Peters had the look of a consummate baseball executive. He arrived at the ballpark first thing in the morning, sporting his tan, daytime suits, Oxford shirts, and striped ties, with his dark brown hair already beginning to gray near the edge of his face. So he slicked it back, revealing his tall forehead, whose wrinkles and lines served as a reminder of his four decades of major-league service.

Peters' first baseball employment was in the minor-league department of the St. Louis Browns in 1946. By 1964, he was appointed by volatile Kansas City A's owner Charlie O. Finley to serve as his general manager. After his work with the A's, Peters presided over the National Association from 1971 to 1975, then joined the O's, taking the club to a league pennant in '79 and a World Series victory in '83. But the O's capped off their 1987 campaign in sixth place in the AL East at 67–95, making it two consecutive years that the club finished the season with a losing record.

Williams called Peters into his office the next morning to inform him that he would be relieved from his position, citing "philosophical differences" as the grounds for his dismissal. But it didn't take long for other teams to show an interest in his services. His track record in the front office made him a desirable hire. Moreover, his staffs had a reputation for their knack for scouting talent, and that was a trait that intrigued Dick Jacobs.

Hank's scouts were responsible for signing Rollie Fingers to his first professional contract in Kansas City, long before the Hall of Fame pitcher ever sported his now famous handlebar mustache. Hank had also taken Reggie Jackson with the second overall pick in the 1966 amateur draft. *If only he could bring the same caliber of All-Star talent to Cleveland and duplicate those successes,* Jacobs thought. So he summoned Peters to Cleveland, sending his personal aircraft to pick him up. Hank was very familiar with the city, having worked there from 1965–71 as director of player personnel and assistant general manager under former president and part owner Gabe Paul. His responsibilities then included the Indians' farm system and scouting departments, but that was then. Now, Hank was sixty-three years old. He wasn't ready to retire, but he was well aware of the organization's pitfalls; primarily the fact that the Indians leased Municipal Stadium from the Browns, who limited their share of money from advertising space around the park. The lack of fan interest didn't scare him away, but it could have been crippling to the franchise, as ticket sales were the team's only significant source of income. It would prevent him from being able to offer appealing contracts to established players on the free agent market. "This was all taking place before television and radio participation in local and national markets made money for the have-nots, as well as the haves," he notes. The farm system also needed serious revamping. Given the financial limitations, the organization would have to find and develop its own talent. That combination of factors alone put Hank in no position to promise Jacobs and the city of Cleveland a championship franchise anytime soon. He went so far as to tell the Jacobs brothers that he would not be fielding a winning team during his tenure there.

"It wasn't like I went in with a rosy outlook," Peters recalls. "I went in with a very realistic outlook."

What he could offer was to at least give them a scheme for building a foundation around which they could win in the future; starting with player-personnel development and scouting. He could also give them a framework to shape business operations and public relations so that their achievements extended off the field, as well as on it.

The Jacobs brothers liked how that sounded and offered Peters the job. He accepted, saying that he would be finished at the end of his contract. "I told them, 'I'm not gonna be here forever. I'll stay for three, maybe four years. What I'll try to do is build a foundation for you and assemble a staff that I think is capable of doing the job, so that when I do leave, it will hopefully be in good hands.'"

He could say so confidently. Along with foregoing the final two years of his contract, Williams also purged the office personnel from Peters' staff. The Orioles released the director of scouting and player development, Tom Giordano, an hour before they booted the general manager. Williams had contemplated letting Giordano go a year or two after winning the '83 World Series, but Peters was in his corner and made the owner keep him on staff. Giordano was Peters' longtime associate in Baltimore and a baseball lifer. He was the first person Peters called after he was let go, and he was the first person he thought to bring with him when he reported for work in November.

* * *

Tom Giordano's given name was Carmine. He changed it to Tommy at the urging of a scout named Jack Egan, who signed him to his first professional contract. Egan had to persuade Giordano's parents that the correct thing for their son to do was to anglicize his name.

"Baseball wasn't ready for an infielder named Carmine Giordano," he recalled Egan saying.

That wouldn't matter much anyways. Everyone around the sport knew Giordano as "T-Bone." He earned his nickname because he routinely ate a cut of porterhouse steak from his father's grocery store in Newark, New Jersey, before playing his high school games in the early forties. His father, who ventured across the Atlantic Ocean from his native Italy, cooked a T-bone steak in a hand grate over the fire in the basement for his son, while his mother made a salad and fresh-baked bread. His grandfather slipped him a glass of 7-Up and added a splash of homemade Italian red wine to wash down the meal before returning to the baseball field.

The Red Sox signed Giordano out of high school, but a fastball to the head brought his first stint of professional baseball to a halt. Giordano enrolled at Panzer College of Physical Education, which later merged with Montclair State University in New Jersey. Panzer did not belong to the National Collegiate Athletic Association, so Giordano played three seasons before signing again with Egan—this time to play for the Pittsburgh Pirates.

All those steaks at lunchtime helped Giordano make a name for himself as a power-hitting infielder. He led the South Atlantic League in 1953 with 24 home runs—two more than Jacksonville's Hank Aaron. Giordano reached the major leagues with the Philadelphia Athletics at the end of the season, but retired as a player in 1954 after playing in only 11 games. After retirement, he managed in the minor leagues before Hank Peters hired him to be his scout for the greater New York area.

The two worked together for the Athletics and for the duration of Peters' tenure with the Orioles. They famously selected baseball's "Iron Man," Cal Ripken Jr., in the second round of the 1978 amateur draft.

* * *

In spite of their accomplishments, Hank Peters and Tom Giordano knew that their time in Baltimore would eventually elapse. Tom called Hank after being fired and was astonished to learn that both of them had been released. Hank, however, told him not to worry, because he was going to make him second to his command with the Indians. The club introduced Giordano as the assistant to the president.

Peters also brought Giordano's assistant from Baltimore, Dan O'Dowd, to become the minor league club director. O'Dowd had joined the Orioles as a twenty-three-year-old and worked in the club's broadcasting and marketing departments before Hank promoted him as the assistant director of player development and scouting. Bringing O'Dowd along helped the Indians start building the club in what the front office felt was the right direction.

After his first season in Cleveland, where the team lost 101 games, Peters realized that he was still not at all satisfied with the Indians' business operations. He looked for somebody to spearhead the club's new business approach; somebody who had experience in baseball operations with the know-how for running a team. He started checking around with friends he knew in other front offices for recommendations. Bill Giles and David Montgomery of the Philadelphia Phillies suggested one of their own, Dennis Lehmann. The executives mentored Lehmann during his eighteen years working with the club. He was serving as the director of marketing and would certainly make for a good fit in Peters' front office.

"Dennis brought a lot of ideas he wanted to incorporate into the Indians' organization, and he helped change the mindset of people so that we weren't just existing," stated Peters. "He helped us become an organization on the rise."

Peters also brought back Bob DiBiasio, a native Clevelander and a former Indians employee, to head the club's public relations department. "Bobby D." knew his way around town and could help the team refine its image better than anyone else.

With this capable staff in place, Dick Jacobs felt comfortable tiptoeing into meetings with his front office staff and sneaking into a chair in the back of the room. Peters would stop to allow the owner to speak, but Jacobs would say, "Don't mind me," and let the brains behind his operation rebuild the franchise. Their first order of business: restocking the farm system.

Chapter Four

HANK'S EARLY DRAFTS

At the time of Hank Peters' arrival in Cleveland, the general consensus among baseball executives was that being thrifty was not the answer for immediate contention. In fact, the most competitive clubs were busy pushing stacks of cash across the negotiating table to sign players. That's the way the game had been ever since the Yankees signed Jim "Catfish" Hunter, the reigning Cy Young Award winner, to a record-setting $3.75-million contract heading into the 1975 season. Hunter became the highest-paid player in the game and the first veteran player in history to change teams as a free agent. *Baseball Prospectus* buttresses this argument over teams' spending habits, noting that four of the five highest payrolls in 1989 belonged to the 1988 division winners: Boston Red Sox, Oakland A's, New York Mets, and Los Angeles Dodgers. Ironically, the Yankees were the outliers. George Steinbrenner spent $18,482,251—the second most in the AL—to field his team, and New York finished with a losing record of 74–87 in 1989.

The Indians knew that it was not yet their time in the late eighties to follow the league's most competitive teams and splurge on six- and seven-figure contracts. The practice of spending freely was far less agreeable to the organization in those years. Dick Jacobs was not eager to spend, though the owner would have offered Hank *cart blanche* "with a ceiling" to sign talent if he felt it was necessary. However, the front office recognized that the franchise was not at a point at which it would have been appropriate to ask its owner to dig deeper into his pockets to ink players to enticing deals or landing overpriced veterans or All-Stars whose perceived value was inflated by their superstardom. That went against the grain with their business strategy. Accordingly, Cleveland continued to play as a thrifty ball club on a dime budget. Just one other club in the AL spent less money on its team in 1989, and only the Chicago White Sox and Detroit Tigers finished with worse records.[1]

Of course, all this did was make fulfilling Hank's promises to Dick a little easier. He reminded the owner that there was an unmistaken correlation between the size of the payroll and the measure of success on the field, and, consequently, he never turned out a winning product in Cleveland during his tenure as general manager. The club never finished better than eleven games out of first place, for that matter, and it dropped 105 games in 1991, as he left the franchise for retirement. But the objective of Hank's involvement had much less to do with the performance of the big-league Indians, and more on the franchise as a whole. The supply of talent developing at the club's minor-league affiliates was meager at best when Hank's group arrived. Apart from their young slugger, Albert Belle, the rest of the farm system showed little promise. Dick brought in Hank to renew the organization's commitment to developing the team's foundation down on the farm, as doing so would allow the Indians to maximize their profits in the long run. It was very much in line with the investor's mantra, "Buy low, sell high."

The Indians couldn't spend any less than on minor-league contracts, and the club's scouting programs could best serve the franchise in stockpiling

---

[1] The Chicago White Sox spent less ($8,565,410) and finished at 69–92. The Detroit Tigers, whose payroll was in the middle of the league ($15,669,304), finishing at 59–103. Seattle spent a hair more than the Indians (third lowest, $10,099,500) and had the same record (73–89).

the farm system with able-bodied players through the entry draft in June. Surely there would be some ballplayers who wouldn't pan out while they sported Chief Wahoo on their sleeves; after all, scouting isn't exactly infallible. There was still plenty of risk and reward to factor in signing high school and college-level prospects.

In evaluation, college talent seemed to be a safer bet. Players with years of intercollegiate experience were more developed—both physically and technically—than their prep counterparts. Most high school players' raw physical attributes and tools, the most valuable being speed and power, would not compare to those of the average collegian. Furthermore, players with NCAA experience could be evaluated using a larger sample of comprehensive statistics measured against a more advanced level of competition. This helped to standardize hitter production and pitcher performance before the draft. Clubs could learn from a batter's home run or strikeout rate in college, as well as the scouts' assessments that he had a nice, short swing and made strong contact. In other words, clubs knew, for the most part, what they were getting from college players because their play translated more congruently to the next level. In contrast, there was still plenty of upside to drafting kids out of high school. They could see the benefit of professional instruction earlier into their careers and get into the ballplayer routine quicker than college players, who still had to take time out of their schedules to attend classes and study for exams. High schoolers also tended to be more pliable as well, and would be easier to mold to an organization's liking.

* * *

Cleveland's first-round stocks from Hank's early drafts looked less than promising in the short run. Hank's first scouting director, Chet Montgomery, selected Mark Lewis, a shortstop and the second overall pick, as the club's top choice in 1988. Lewis would hop around the league for eleven years, switching teams seven times over that span, and failed to make a strong impact with the Indians. The scouting department redeemed itself when Hank used the

Indians' supplemental first-round pick on Charles Nagy, a right-hander from the University of Connecticut, who made three All-Star teams and went on to enjoy thirteen seasons near the top of the Tribe's starting rotation.

Then with the club's top pick in the 1989 draft, they made a complete blunder. Cleveland had the eleventh overall selection and went after a third baseman from W. T. White High School in Dallas, Texas.

Calvin Murray had an athletic profile (his older brother, Kevin, was a former quarterback at Texas A&M who set multiple Aggies passing records) and the Indians' scouting department was optimistic that he would have a successful professional career in its organization. In all actuality, somebody in the scouting department had to have been careless, as Murray had other ideas. Apparently it was common knowledge that he wasn't going to come to Cleveland if the Indians drafted him, meaning that the scout failed at determining his signability. Even after team officials visited Murray and his family at home and upped the ball club's bonus offering, the young athlete ended up passing on the Tribe and took a scholarship offer from the University of Texas to play baseball. Although he eventually went on to enjoy parts of five seasons in the major leagues, Calvin Murray never suited up in an Indians uniform and was a wasted No. 1 pick.

It wasn't until the Indians botched their first-round selection the following year that Chet Montgomery was eventually let go. Chet submitted Tim Costo, a first-team All-American shortstop at Iowa, as his top draft choice. Costo had learned how much the Indians offered Murray to sign the previous year, so the club ended up paying too much to persuade him to sign. Worse, Costo looked awkward in the field, scouts later opined, and had too long of a swing to be effective in the big leagues. He might have hit 21 round-trippers during his award-winning junior season for the Hawkeyes, but Costo would only hit three dingers in his two seasons in the majors.

In hindsight, it is always easier to review draft classes after the fact to spot the gambles that paid off; to see which purported surefire All Stars turned out to be busts and which other players have favorable careers; either in Cleveland or with another organization. Chet's replacement, Mickey White, was quick to point out the value in his predecessor's drafts. Certainly the organization had less luck with its higher-profile selections, but some of the Indians' better picks came later in the later rounds.

"You may trip up on the first one and say, 'Okay, sometimes that's the way things happen,'" White recalls. "But look at the pure numbers of guys that Chet got that became very successful major-league players and were an integral part of the teams of the nineties. Forget about that No. 1 for a second and look at his leadership ring: Chet brought fifteen to eighteen guys who played in the big leagues after he was there. He got star players and signed them."

For example, Montgomery took Jerry Dipoto (pitcher), Jesse Levis (catcher), Alan Embree (pitcher), Curt Leskanic (pitcher), Kelly Stinnett (catcher), and Brian Giles (outfielder) between the third and seventeenth rounds in 1989. All of those players became bona fide major leaguers. Those selections would later become overshadowed by the Indians' pick in the thirteenth round; a "shortstop" from Illinois Central College named Jim Thome.

Chapter Five

DRAFTING THOME

Scouting Report

From the Desk of Tom Couston

*"Inside-out swing at this point . . . willingly uses the opposite field. . . .
Excellent power potential if he learns to turn on the ball . . . could easily
add weight and muscle to 200-pound frame. Works hard at defense,
but may not have the range to stay at third base. . . . High-character
guy. Comes from strong blue-collar family."*

If it wasn't for Chet Montgomery acting on the gut instincts of his Midwest-area scout, baseball might have never been introduced to one of its most prolific home-run hitters. It's something that even the slugger admits. The scout was Tom Couston,[1] and the boy he saw on a scouting trip to Limestone Community High School in Peoria County, Illinois, was not unlike any of the thousands of other teenaged players he had seen as he scoured dusty ball fields around Middle America for talent. Jim Thome had dreams of becoming a big leaguer just like the rest of them.

---

[1] Couston's last name is modified from his family's Greek surname, Kostopanagiotis. In addition to signing Thome, Couston later signed RHP Jeremy Hellickson and CF Kevin Kiermaier for the Tampa Bay Rays.

"Jimmy doesn't forget where he came from," says Couston. It's true enough that the scout was invited to sit with Thome's father at U. S. Cellular Field in Chicago to watch as the slugger hit career home run No. 500 on September 16, 2007.

The largest city on the Illinois River, Peoria is so representative of the average American city that it has been referenced historically as a standard for mainstream Midwestern culture. The question, "Will it play in Peoria?" was so often asked about acts on the Vaudeville theater circuit at the turn of the twentieth century that the meaning of the phrase was eventually generalized to address the appeals of the American people as a whole. It's only fitting that Jim, the youngest of Chuck Jr. and Joyce Thome's five children, came from a pedigree of softball players enshrined in the Greater Peoria Sports Hall of Fame to honor the multi-generational achievements on the diamond by his father, Grandfather Chuck Sr., Uncle Art, and Aunt Carolyn. By the time he was eight, Jim announced to his mother that he was never going to work and that he was going to play baseball in the big leagues.

If he couldn't round up the neighborhood kids for a game, Jim picked up an aluminum bat and hit white rocks from the driveway of the family home. He tried smacking the rocks the same way his idol, Chicago Cubs long-ball specialist Dave Kingman, crushed baseballs. Jim grew up watching the Cubs on WGN and lauded "Kong" for his tape-measure home runs that often soared past the bleachers and beyond the friendly confines of Wrigley Field, crashing through the windows of the apartments facing the ballpark along Waveland Avenue with reckless disregard.

Jim once tried to get an autograph from Kingman when his dad took him to his first Cubs game. They drove about 150 miles from Chicago and had seats near the dugout. After Kingman snubbed his request during batting practice, the nine-year-old Thome vaulted over a wall, found his way through the dugout, and headed toward the clubhouse, determined to meet his favorite slugger. Barry Foote, the Cubs' catcher, stopped Jim and returned him to his father, but not before he handed the boy a baseball signed by some of his teammates. The brief encounter in the dugout only reinforced the idea that Jim wanted nothing more than to become a major leaguer.

Thome had not yet filled out his 6-foot-4-inch, 250-pound frame when Couston saw him for the first time in high school. Jim was lanky and had a sunken chest. Just by looking at his limbs and torso, the scout could tell he still had room to develop into a burly power-hitter. Jim's older brothers were physical guys, and their father was even bigger.

Jim's time running to first base turned away some of the first scouts who evaluated him. It took him almost five seconds to lumber the ninety feet to the bag.[2] He would swing so hard that he often got tied up in the batter's box . . . but that did not scare Couston. Apart from clocking him at 6.8 seconds (a strong average time) in the 60-yard dash, the scout had other indicators to prove that Thome was athletic. He was the leading scorer on his high school basketball team; an All State guard who put up 36 points when Limestone won its league title in triple overtime. Sure, he didn't have the first-step quickness to be a shortstop, but his glove was decent and he threw well enough to keep his bat in the lineup and not be a liability in the field. That factor would be helpful to any suitor, because Jim's bat would certainly be his most intriguing draw. But at that time, there were no suitors. Couston heard that Thome was going to play baseball in junior college, something the scout thought would benefit the young player; therefore, Jim's name was not called on draft day in 1988.

A year passed before Couston saw Thome again; in April of 1989. There were a handful of scouts on hand, but they had all gathered to see another shortstop play against Illinois Central College. Even Couston had come to see the other team's prospect, but spotted Thome and recognized him as the strong kid from Peoria whom he had seen the previous spring. The other scouts paid no attention to him; probably still thinking he was too slow and

---

[2] A time of 4.2 seconds to first base for a left-handed batter is considered average. Five seconds is inferior.

awkward to be a shortstop. Couston, on the other hand, saw much improvement in his game.

Thome already showed signs that he was growing. He was still only eighteen and would have additional time for his body to mature even further. Moreover, he was beginning to look like a major-league hitter in the batter's box. He seemed to have a good idea of the strike zone and exhibited a total sense of control over his body, with enough strength in his arms from his elbows to his wrists to make solid contact. Most kids who swung that hard would often hit the bottom of the baseball and make weaker contact.

The ball also seemed to rise a little off Thome's bat when he connected on pitches. His swing was still occasionally long, which would have deterred some other scouts, but his bat speed and contact made up for it. The stroke was becoming smoother; more compact and plenty more powerful. *With some more at-bats in pro ball, he will develop wrists so strong that he'll finally have loft; the final dimension to becoming a power-hitter and regularly blast towering shots,* Couston thought.

Thome made four outs in as many plate appearances that day, but, as the scout noted, they came off his bat with such force that they could have taken the heads off the infielders. Impressed, Couston decided that he would approach him after the game. He walked up to the coach and asked him to send over his shortstop to talk, but the coach brought over the wrong kid. *Jeez, nobody must want to talk to this guy.* Thome eventually came over, and to avoid tipping off any of the remaining scouts lingering by the field that he was interested, Couston resorted to one of his favorite tricks. He instructed Thome to keep his back to him. The scout did the same.

"I want to talk to you, but don't look me in the eye," Couston said.

This confused Thome. He thought he might have done something wrong, but followed the scout's directions and started looking around the ball field.

"Do you want to play professional baseball?" Couston asked.

Thome turned his attention back to the scout.

"Quit lookin' at me!" he snapped.

Thome immediately turned back around and nodded, "Yes, sir, I do."

That was the scout's cue to introduce himself.

"My name is Tom Couston and I'm a scout from the Indians. I'm gonna come back and see you. I'm not gonna talk to you, but I'll be talking to you before the draft."

That was it. The exchange couldn't have lasted any longer, or else the other scouts might have caught on. Thome still laughs about Couston's sly scouting tactics more than twenty years later. But at the onset of his major-league journey, he was just pleased to be considered as one of the club's future draft selections.

Chapter Six

THE JOHN HART EXPERIMENT

Hank Peters was tired. Whenever he felt drowsy, the general manager would close his door, put his feet up on his desk, and close his eyes for twenty minutes in the middle of the day. That was his secret to lasting four decades in baseball. But less than a week before his sixty-fifth birthday, in the beginning of September 1989, the Indians' 65–78 record put them in second-to-last place in the American League East. In addition to feeling tired, Peters was growing frustrated. Whenever that would happen, he called Tom Giordano into his office.

"We're going to have to make a move at the major-league level," Peters said.

That meant the skipper, Doc Edwards, was about to become unemployed. Doc had been the bullpen coach when Joe Klein, the former vice president of baseball operations, tapped him to replace Pat Corrales midway through the 1987 season. His managerial style was a welcomed change, compared to that of his predecessor. Pat Tabler, the Indians' lone representative at the '89 All-Star Game, had told reporters that Doc was the type of manager whose door was always open; something which sat especially well with his players. Corrales, in contrast, was an oppressor who required his players to wear helmets when they took batting practice and outlawed card games in the clubhouse.

In any case, Doc Edwards' hire didn't result in any significant improvement, and after a year and a half, it led Peters to make a managerial switch.

"Tell Doc we're not bringing him back, and get some names together," he told Giordano.

Giordano already had an immediate replacement in mind; somebody within the organization that he had been grooming long before he and Hank ever arrived in Cleveland.

* * *

Tom Giordano discovered John Hart on a scouting trip to Florida while working with the Baltimore Orioles in 1982. Giordano's daughter Gail taught physical education at Colonial High School in Orlando, and she kept telling him about the competitive baseball teams at Boone High School. Hart, who coached the Boone Braves, led the team to a State Championship in 1981.[1] Giordano's scout in the area, Jack Sanford, raved about the school's catcher, Ron Karkovice, and said he should watch him play.

Understand that Giordano was very particular about traveling to evaluate players for Baltimore. There was a chain of command that needed to be followed. His scouts reported to assistants, who reported back to him. They ranked prospects and players on lists, and he went to scout them in order of his preference. Boone's backstop was a six-footer with a strong, athletic build. He topped the list the assistants submitted, so Tom and Jack went to see him play at a night game in 1982.

---

[1] John Hart was elected to the Boone High School Hall of Fame from his work as their baseball head coach in 2002.

They got to the field around four o'clock, long before any other spectators arrived. A noise coming out of the locker room caught Giordano's attention: the sound of baseball spikes crunching on pavement. He looked toward the dugout and saw the team, led by its manager, marching to the field. These high school ball players looked like professionals. Their uniforms were spotless. They took a lap around the field and circled their manager for a word before breaking into calisthenics and warm-up exercises. They had the right throwing mechanics. They played pepper games. Pepper games! *You hardly saw that anymore.*[2] Hart threw batting practice exactly the way they did in pro ball, forcing his players to spray the ball to all fields with situational hitting drills.

Once the game started, the manager positioned himself in the third-base coaching box, a la Los Angeles Dodgers skipper Tommy Lasorda. He relayed elaborate signs to base runners as they established their leads. His first-base coach waved his arms for batters to make the turn for second even on base hits, calling for the runners to retreat only after the ball was fielded cleanly.

The game ended and Sanford asked Giordano what he thought about Hart's catcher. Karkovice played a good defensive game, but he didn't hit well enough to be considered as one of his top choices.[3] But Giordano was more interested in meeting the manager.

Surprised, Sanford asked, "Pray tell, boss man, why do you want to meet that young fellow?"

Giordano was impressed by Hart's baseball abilities and his maturity, and it turned out that there was good reason for it. John Hart had been an All-American at Seminole Junior College and caught in the Montreal Expos organization for three years before returning home to pursue a degree at the

---

[2] Pepper is a game where one player hits ground balls to a group of fielders who are standing close by.

[3] The Chicago White Sox ended up drafting Karkovice in the first round a few months later.

University of Central Florida in history and physical education. He wanted to stay around baseball after finishing school, and so he took the coaching job at Boone. Giordano tracked him down after the game and asked him to meet for lunch the next day.

At their appointment, Giordano told him, "John, I don't have a job open at this time for you, but I'm tremendously impressed with your baseball abilities. You are a people person, and you need that, especially if you are going to work with young players."

Giordano continued. "So this is what I have in mind. I'm going to offer you something."

John looked at him, intrigued.

"I've never heard of any scouting director ever offering this kind of a deal. I'm offering you a guaranteed two-year contract. That means if I make a mistake on this, you're still going to keep earning money for two years, non-negotiable."

John had to think about the man's offer. He had a family of his own in Florida, and Baltimore was almost 1,000 miles away. He had already turned down offers to return to professional baseball in the past, and, in fact, ended up turning down Giordano's initial offer to become a scout for the Orioles. But for the last six weeks of the school year, after he had fulfilled his baseball obligations at Boone, John Hart attended games with Jack Sanford to evaluate players who weren't his own. Sanford vetted Hart and reported his thoughts back to Giordano. When the Orioles had an opening for a manager at their rookie-ball team in Bluefield, West Virginia, they offered the position to Hart. He and his wife, Sandi, met with Giordano for dinner and finalized the deal.

In his first season as a minor-league manager, Rookie-level won the Appalachian League title, a feat it had not accomplished in eleven years. The Orioles promoted John to their Class-A affiliate in Hagerstown, Maryland, where he stayed for two years. His next stops were at Double-A and Triple-A for two more seasons. He even did a stint in the Dominican Republic before earning a promotion to become the third-base coach for the major-league team. By then, Giordano had already followed Peters to Cleveland.

* * *

The Indians had already come calling to interview John Hart before, but Baltimore owner Edward Bennett Williams denied him permission to talk to the club, promising him that he was on tap to take over as the Orioles' next manager. But Williams died that summer, which cleared the way for Hank Peters to invite John to join the Cleveland organization for the 1989 season.

"I remember thinking, at that time, that Hank was going to want me to manage the club," recalls Hart. After all, that's what he had been used to doing. Instead, Hank offered him a position as a front-office assistant, where he would have input on the players, the hiring of staff, and setting the vision for what the Indians would put on the field. Peters encouraged him to take it.

"With your ability to communicate and your field background, this is going to be great. I can teach you the other pieces of it," he said.

John agreed to move to Cleveland, where he found himself working for the first time in a front office. When he arrived at Municipal Stadium, he stopped at his secretary's desk and introduced himself. Ethel LaRue was mild-mannered, astute, and very good on the phone. She was a seasoned baseball secretary.

"Ethel, I've never worked in a front office. I don't even know how to work the phone system," Hart said.

She gave him a reassuring laugh and said, "When these buttons ring, you tell me what to do."

He could handle that.

In Cleveland, John also found himself working again under Tom. He sent Hart around the majors as a special assignment scout, a role that allowed him to grow familiar with front-office circles and gave him a chance to develop contacts in every city around the league.

But John Hart was only Tom Giordano's short-term solution for Hank Peters to fill the big-league field manager's role. There would be a point at which Peters was no longer going to be the general manager, and Giordano didn't want the job, either. He was only a year younger than Hank, and even after taking extra vitamins, his eyesight wasn't as good as it once was. He had no interest in the position. John, on the other hand, would make an exceptional fit in that role.

"John is credentialed for any job you want to give him," Giordano said. "He's proved it in our system, and in Baltimore, and even before that in high school. He's impressed me. And he's going to come in and ask me, 'Damn it, T-Bone, why won't you give me a shot to manage?' Come next season, the answer is going to be no."

Hank stared from across the desk, contemplating Giordano's every word.

"Henry, you're the general manager. When John is assigned, it's coming from you." He continued, "You called the other GMs, introducing him as the advance scout. He's been talking to them, finding out what they need. He's done a good job. Now get off that damn wagon. Everything is set for you: John Hart is the fellow after you go."

And just like that, Hank Peters and Tom Giordano called in John Hart with 19 games remaining in the 1989 season and asked him how he felt about managing the club until the end of the year. As they expected, he was eager when he delivered his response.

"Oh, yeah, absolutely!" Then Giordano cut in.

"This is with the understanding, John, that it's only until the end of the year. Even if you win every game, you're not to come in here and tell me that you want to be interviewed. After this, your job will not be on the field any longer."

Hank echoed, "John, this is right up your alley. You're going to have a lot more input on the baseball piece of it because you can not only get the players. You can hire the staff and set the vision for what you want to see on the field."

John didn't need any more convincing, and he quickly accepted. He was issued a uniform and headed straight for the dugout. The Indians went 8–11 during that 19-game stretch, after which John handed the control of the lineup card over to John McNamara, and took over as the director of baseball operations for the club. There he would remain until Peters' retirement in September of 1991, at which point he would be tapped to succeed Hank as the Indians' next general manager.

Chapter Seven

THE JOE CARTER TRADE

"Sandy Alomar Jr., Carlos Baerga, and Chris James from San Diego
for Joe Carter? That's the deal that started it all."

—Paul Hoynes, Indians beat writer, *Cleveland Plain Dealer*

In the weeks leading up to the 1989 Winter Meetings in Nashville, Tennessee, Hank Peters was faced with an objective: finding a new home for outfielder Joe Carter. This was something the general manager had hoped to accomplish by the time he and his staff left the Gaylord Opryland Resort and Convention Center at the conclusion of the annual meetings. Hank, like many Indians executives before him, was not seeking to trade his superstar because he wanted to. Instead, he had to make the move out of necessity. Cleveland, over time, had become a revolving door. The Indians had a longstanding practice of dealing top veteran players before the end of their contracts, as they did not want those players to walk away from the club as free agents and be left empty-handed. The team was never in the financial position to re-sign its reputable players to substantial contract extensions, especially when the team wasn't at the top of the standings. As a result, men like Hank Peters had to execute trades that resulted in All-Stars leaving town more frequently than the other way around. The trades, however, would at least ensure that they would get some players in return. Think of it as a form of addition by subtraction. Unfortunately, it was a fundamental part of why the club had trouble keeping its fan base: Everyone's beloved Indians players were being shipped out of town as soon as they gained their following.

That was the case with Carter, too. Joe Carter, an outfielder and first baseman, had a breakout year in 1984—his second major-league season—after the Chicago Cubs traded him to Cleveland, and turned into one of the top home run hitters in the American League.[1] From 1986 to '89, he averaged 30 home runs and 108 runs batted in per year. He was also skilled on the base paths, compiling as many as 31 stolen bases in 1987. (That was the same year he appeared on the cover of *Sports Illustrated* with Cory Snyder.)

Carter had just hit a career-best 35 home runs and earned $1.63 million in 1989. He was twenty-nine years old, would be eligible for arbitration in 1990, and could declare for free agency in 1991. That was right around the corner. Peters wanted to sign him to an extension, and went back and forth with Carter's agent trying to negotiate a deal. Each of his proposals to the agent, Jim Turner, was immediately shot down. In turn, the general manager rejected Turner's counteroffer, and after the 1989 season, Peters made a final pitch to the slugger for a three-year deal worth $10 million. With this rejection, Peters stopped his negotiations and released a statement, declaring that Carter would be traded by the year's end. Carter's bat was worth a few bona fide prospects, which would help the GM address some legitimate roster needs.

Now because Carter was about to enter the final year of his existing contract with Cleveland, any team that acquired him would consequently want him to sign an extension before completing a trade with the Indians. What complicated things was a stipulation Carter made through his agent;

---

[1] In the trade, the Indians sent Joe Carter, Mel Hall, Don Schulze, and minor leaguer Darryl Banks to Chicago for Rick Sutcliffe, George Frazier, and Ron Hassey.

he would only agree to long-term extensions with five teams: the California Angels, St. Louis Cardinals, Los Angeles Dodgers, San Diego Padres, or Kansas City Royals. This clause reduced many trade scenarios that otherwise could have been viable options for Peters.

A week before the Winter Meetings, Carter, too, weighed his options. He liked Kansas City as a first choice, but he also called the Padres' outfielder Tony Gwynn, who tried to sell him on San Diego. The Padres had finished ahead of the Dodgers and trailed the San Francisco Giants by three games in the final National League standings, completing the season with an 89–73 record. However, a move to San Diego wasn't going to be all sunshine and palm trees; housing prices there were steep, and Carter wanted to be sure he could get a lucrative deal wherever he ended up.

In the meantime, the Indians also considered their needs. Cleveland was in the market for a catcher. Andy Allanson, their primary backstop, had proven to be respectable behind the plate. At 6-foot-5 and 220 pounds, Allanson was a redwood of a man. Despite having the frame of a lumber-jack (minus the beard), he wasn't exactly equipped with Paul Bunyan-like strength in the batter's box. Allanson's bat had as much charge as a soggy firecracker and as much pop as a Hall-less Oates. It took him over one thousand at-bats before he hit his first professional home run, which prompted pitcher Phil Niekro to lie on his back and feign shock in the dugout. Allanson never hit more than five long balls in a season, and in his eight-year career with almost 1,500 at-bats, only totaled 16. Other options behind the plate included Rick Dempsey, who was past his prime, and Joel Skinner, a career backup. There had even been talk at one point of converting the young Jim Thome into a catcher, but that never materialized.

As the Indians contemplated a potential trade with San Diego, their lack of depth behind the plate led them to develop a particular interest in Sandy Alomar Jr., a catching prospect in the Padres organization who had been twice named Minor League Player of the Year in consecutive seasons by *Baseball America*.

There was little opportunity for Sandy to play in the big leagues with the Padres.[2] Benito Santiago was already handling the everyday catching duties, and in three full seasons in San Diego had won the Rookie of the Year Award (1987), back-to-back Silver Sluggers (1987 and '88), and a pair of Gold Gloves (1988 and '89). He made his first trip to the All-Star Game in 1989, starting for the National League. Padres general manager Jack McKeon knew this, too, and saw it as an opportunity for both clubs to benefit.

The two sides negotiated. San Diego wanted to give Cleveland an outfielder, Chris James, who, with the trade, would be joining his third pro team in five years. His home run totals were in the teens, and the Indians factored him into the lineup picture primarily as a designated hitter or utility player. The Indians were also asking for McKeon to include in their offer Carlos Baerga, a minor-league third baseman from Santurce, Puerto Rico. This slowed the negotiating, as the Padres' GM was less eager to throw Baerga into the deal. Carlos Baerga had surged through the San Diego farm system, hitting at every level on the way up. It took him three seasons to reach Triple-A Las Vegas; when he arrived, the twenty-year-old hit .275 with 10 homers and 74 runs batted in over 132 games for the Stars.[3] McKeon mulled the decision into the wee hours of the morning. Peters and his front office waited, and to their delight, McKeon relented, agreeing to a trade that included Baerga by 1 a.m. The deal became official on December 6, 1989, and the next day, Carter signed a three-year extension with the Padres worth $9.2 million.

---

[2] One of Sandy Jr.'s teammates with the Padres was his brother Roberto, who, like their father, was already developing into an All-Star second baseman.

[3] The Stars later became the Las Vegas 51s in 2001.

Chapter Eight

RICK WOLFF AND THE PSYCHOLOGY OF WINNING

Rick Wolff received a phone call from a number he didn't recognize in December of 1989, shortly after the conclusion of the Winter Meetings. On the line was Harvey Dorfman, whose books, *The ABC's of Pitching: A Handbook for Performance Enhancement* and *The Mental Game of Baseball: A Guide to Peak Performance*, had landed him a job with the Oakland A's, that year's World Series champion and the winner of the last two American League pennants. His books were regarded as the Athletics' paperback bibles.

Word had gotten out about Oakland's radical psychological approach to baseball, and it drummed up interest in mental skills coaching among the other teams at the briefings. There were only a precious few mental skills coaches with professional organizations at that time, and guys who could give teams a psychological edge like Harvey Dorfman did were in demand. Dorfman read Wolff's guide, *The Psychology of Winning Baseball: A Coach's Handbook*, and was calling to inform him that teams would be interested in him, too. This caught Rick off guard. While he was flattered that some guy he didn't know had read his work, he was still skeptical of the notion that a major league franchise would seriously consider bringing him on board.

Then, again, Rick had some legitimate credentials. He played second base at Harvard, leaving the Ivy League after the Detroit Tigers took him late in the 1972 draft, and spent two seasons playing for single-A affiliates before deciding to call it quits. After that, he focused on writing.

But Wolff couldn't stay away from the game. He served as an assistant coach at Pace University and managed the Division-II program at Mercy College in Dobbs Ferry, New York, bringing the Flyers to a national ranking. He also did color commentary for ESPN at the 1986 College World Series, and even made a brief return as a player three years later, joining the South Bend White Sox for three games in 1989. Rick hit a double and drove in three runs, faring 4–7 against Midwest League pitchers. Not a bad showing for a thirty-eight-year-old who had taken a fifteen-year hiatus from the game as a player. *Sports Illustrated* even featured the article he wrote about the experience.

Wolff gave Dorfman the okay to forward his contact information to clubs, and within a week, he had received calls from six teams. The Indians were one of the first to call. Rick was introduced to Hank Peters, his young heir apparent, John Hart, and their minor league director, Dan O'Dowd. They wanted him to join the organization as a roving instructor. He would work with the players, help them refine a mental edge, and try to improve their performances as they were translated onto the field.

There was nothing glamorous about doing it in Cleveland. America was still laughing at the antics of the Indians on the silver screen after the April release of *Major League* satirized the club's shortcomings and its institution of losing.[1] But something struck him about Peters and his young execs running the real-life Cleveland Indians. He could sense that they were hungry. He told that to his wife as a justification for signing his contract.

Wolff heard from Dorfman again before he reported to Tucson for spring training in 1990, who had more advice for him.

---

[1] In fact, Dick Jacobs flew a handful of players to the movie premiere to get some free publicity out of it.

"You need to be in uniform, to throw batting practice, to hit fungoes, and to walk the outfield as guys are shagging flies. Let them know you were a professional ballplayer and that you have been there. You're not another guy in a suit and tie. They won't open up to you, otherwise."

Rick heeded the suggestion and found that Harvey's advice worked. He also made a pledge of confidentiality to players on certain things, like doctors do for patients. If a guy approached him with concerns that he couldn't hit a curveball, or if a catcher had anxiety throwing the ball back to the pitcher with runners on base, it came with the understanding that those discussions remained between the two of them. Rick required the front office to honor that clause as a condition of his services, which Hank and the staff understood was necessary to help their young players in their development.

Chapter Nine

JOHNNY MAC

The Indians opened the 1990 season with John McNamara as the team's skipper. Johnny Mac was an introvert, a devout Catholic, and a man who never tired on his loyalty to close friends, which included Hank Peters and Tom Giordano. They became acquainted in 1960 when the team McNamara managed in Lewiston, Idaho, was merged into the Kansas City Athletics' system as a Class-B affiliate. When McNamara reported to his first spring training with the Athletics in Daytona Beach, Florida, he was integrated into a growing social group within the organization that would later refer to itself as the Raiders. The collection of managers, scouts, and assorted personnel from the various ranks of the A's operation that comprised the Raiders frequented bars, clubs, and restaurants in town during their spare time, often playing harmless pranks on each other.

Some of the original Raiders included:

Robbie Robertson, a minor-league manager in the A's organization.

Bobby Hofman, who spent seven years as a utility player for fiery skipper Leo Durocher and his New York Giants, and was a part of the 1954 club that swept Cleveland in the World Series. Hofman managed in the minors until

Alvin Dark added him to his big-league staff with the A's in 1966. He went on to work with the Senators, Indians, and Yankees into the 1980s.

Bill Posedel, whose career as a right-hander for the Brooklyn Dodgers and Boston Braves had been interrupted by World War II. "Barnacle Bill" returned to baseball after serving in the Navy from 1942 to 1945, and worked as a scout for the A's in the early sixties before taking over as the big-league pitching coach in 1968.

The group also enjoyed the company of:

Haywood Sullivan, once an All-Southeastern Conference quarterback and a standout catcher at the University of Florida, who floated between the minors and the big leagues with Boston and Kansas City before finally managing in the A's organization. He later returned to the Red Sox as an executive and general partner.

Whitey Herzog, who retired from playing in 1963 and scouted with the A's for two years before joining the Mets as a third-base coach in 1966. Herzog enjoyed a Hall of Fame career as a manager, winning one World Series (1982) and another two National League pennants (1985 and '87) with the St. Louis Cardinals in the eighties.

Of course, Giordano went along for the outings and participated in the shenanigans. It was all in good fun, they told Hank Peters, but he insisted that he be spared the details of their escapades. The group remained friends and reminisced about the times in Daytona even after its members had scattered around the country with their baseball work.

In the twenty years since they had all been united in the same organization, John McNamara bounced from one major league job to another, never stopping in a city for more than four seasons at a time. His travels took him to three teams in his native California, including the A's, Padres, and later, the Angels. He managed the Cincinnati Reds and earned his first playoff berth in 1979, losing the National League pennant in three games to the eventual World Series champion Pittsburgh Pirates. His hallmark campaign came in 1986, when he helped the

Red Sox to the American League pennant and was named AL Manager of the Year. Unfortunately for McNamara, this award was overshadowed by stinging criticisms regarding his decision that contributed to Boston's agonizing defeat by the Mets in the World Series. Writers rebuked him for failing to prevent Bill Buckner's infamous blunder in Game 6. *If only he'd subbed in Dave Stapleton!* some wrote, referring to the first baseman's defensive substitution in Games 1 and 5. Instead, McNamara left Buckner in to play the tenth inning and celebrate winning the championship, when that fateful little roller off the bat of Mookie Wilson bounced up along the first baseline and found its way behind the bag, allowing the winning run to score for the Mets and sending the Series to a decisive Game Seven.

McNamara put the Series defeat in the rearview mirror and was intent on distancing himself from all the noise, but that ultimately was not going to happen in Boston. The Red Sox canned him during the '88 season, and he took a job as an advance scout for the Seattle Mariners.[1]

The relationship Johnny Mac had forged with Peters and Giordano all those years before made him a preferred candidate for the Indians' vacant managerial post when John Hart moved to the front office. He met with Hank on a trip to Cleveland late in the 1989 season, where the two sat and talked about the Indians. With the Tribe again due to finish near the bottom of the barrel in the East, the only place to go was up in the standings. Hank extended him an offer to manage the club in 1990, and McNamara signed on to write the Indians' lineup card for two years.

The actual value of bringing Johnny Mac on board had little to do with improving the Indians' place in the standings, although the club did see a marginal improvement, climbing two spots into fourth place after one season with McNamara in town. Hank's true purpose was that he could count on his old friend to be a steady hand in ensuring progress for the future. The average age on the team's roster was just short of twenty-six years old. Johnny had

---

[1] In three and a half seasons as manager of the Boston Red Sox (1985–88), McNamara posted a 297–273 record (.521 winning percentage), winning one pennant.

plenty of experience developing players in the minors and managing them when they emerged onto the scene in the big leagues, dating back to his time with the A's and Reggie Jackson.

One of the first of McNamara's Indians to emerge was catching prospect Sandy Alomar Jr., who improved behind the plate under Johnny Mac's tutelage. Then again, Sandy was getting the chance to learn from one of the best catching instructors around. McNamara had worked with Johnny Bench in Cincinnati and Bob Boone in California with the Angels, and those two backstops combined for seventeen Gold Glove Awards over the course of their careers. Johnny Mac's philosophy was to give the catcher more control over the pitching staff, reluctant to call pitches from the dugout.

"I always thought the catcher was more involved with the game, as far as sliders or the breaking of a curveball, how good the fastball is moving or how good a change was." He clarifies: "You see more about that from behind the plate than you could from the dugout, unless the catcher is a complete idiot, which, in that case, I'd call pitches from the dugout."

McNamara says that wasn't ever necessary with Sandy. Johnny Mac had full faith and confidence in Alomar's ability to call a game. Even then, he enlisted the help of Joel Skinner, the Indians' veteran catcher, to help Sandy become acclimated. They tipped him off to subtle adjustments of batters' stances and taught him how to change the selection of pitches based on where the hitter stood in the box. It didn't take long for him to get comfortable and to blossom into a starting role in the major leagues.

"Sandy had a great feel for the game and running the pitching staff once he got acclimated," McNamara says.

As a result, Alomar went on to win the 1990 American League Rookie of the Year Award.

Johnny Mac also helped Carlos Baerga transition toward becoming an everyday major-league infielder. Baerga finished out his last year in Triple-A at third base, but came to Cleveland as a utility infielder. In his first season, Baerga saw time predominantly at third base (50 games) and shortstop (48 games). The twenty-one-year-old had his share of defensive struggles—including five errors in eight games at second base—which opened some discussion among the front office staff to send him back to the minors. But that's where Johnny Mac objected. He felt that Baerga would hit and become the next everyday second baseman for the Indians, and that he needed to stay in the big leagues in order for that to happen. He approached Baerga and told him that he would have the opportunity to come in off the bench until he proved himself in the field at second base.

"I want you to be here early every day, and I want you to work out taking ground balls every day to get better," McNamara told him.

The manager's confidence motivated Baerga to put in the work. The following year, Baerga opened the season as the starting third baseman, although he was still a below-average fielder.[2] The only saving grace was that his range at the hot corner was slightly above the league average, and it also translated into his play at second base.[3] By the middle of June, Johnny Mac began to give Baerga more time at second, and it's there that he would eventually stay for the remainder of his time with the Indians.[4]

---

[2] Baerga ended up leading the American League with 27 errors in 1991.

[3] Range factor per nine innings (RF or RF/9) is a defensive metric developed by the noted sabermetrician Bill James. It is a calculation of a player's putouts and assists in a standard nine-inning game. This statistic assumes that a player's participation in making defensive outs is more relevant than his fielding percentage, the most conventional defensive statistics, which measures his ability to cleanly handle batted balls. Fielding percentage does not take into account a player's ability (or the lack thereof) to get to those batted balls. In the case of Carlos Baerga, his RF/9 at third base totaled 3.05 in 1991, which was higher than the league-average 2.75. This index indicated an even better performance when Baerga moved over to second base, where he recorded an RF/9 of 5.7 (compared to the league-average 5.1).

[4] Baerga finished the '91 campaign having made 73 starts at second and recorded a .971 fielding percentage, which was still below the league average, but saw a significant improvement from his limited performance in 1990.

Chapter Ten

THE CONTINUING SAGA OF ALBERT BELLE, PART I

Johnny McNamara's tenure as the Indians' manager may be best remembered for the occasion upon which he demoted young slugger Albert Belle to Triple-A for the "most blatant lack of hustle" he had ever seen, after Belle failed to run out a double play on June 6, 1991, against the Chicago White Sox. That he had been leading the club in home runs and runs batted in at the time would not change the manager's rationale.

"I insisted that ball clubs hustled," McNamara said, defending his position. "I don't expect you to go 110 miles per hour to first base, but at least appear like you're trying. That was more for the fans' sake to show that they hadn't given up."

But despite three or four reminders, that message never got through to Belle; at least not in the bottom of the eighth in a one-run game with a man in scoring position. McNamara was busy watching the lead runner being forced out at third base when he turned and saw the throw to first beat out Belle by three steps.

"What the hell happened there?!" he bellowed at his hitting coach, Jose Morales, who then tried to explain how Belle failed to run out a ground ball yet again. This time, the normally collected McNamara was fuming. When Belle trotted in from left field after the ninth inning, Johnny Mac made his way to the opposite end of the dugout, where he summoned pitcher Tom Candiotti, who at 6-foot-4 was an imposing figure, and Chris James, known for being one of the feistiest of the outfielders.

"Come with me," he commanded them. Truthfully, Johnny Mac didn't know what was going to happen next.

"I thought to myself, *God, what did I get myself into?*" The trio waited for Belle to come down the steps from the field into the dugout, where they expected him to blow by them and head straight for the clubhouse. Mac had other ideas. Just as Belle made his pass, the manager grabbed him by the bicep and said, "Pack your bag, because it's either you or I who's going to be in this dugout tomorrow night and not both of us!"

Johnny Mac was disgusted. The Indians lost the game, 2–1, in ten innings. By the time he got to his office, he found Hank Peters waiting for him, and he was just as fuming. Peters, who was usually very quiet, sent for Belle to come to the office. He sat him across the desk and chewed him out from the other side of the table. When it was over, Belle got up and left without a word.

Tom Giordano had previously made a note of Belle's lack of effort when he scouted him for the Orioles. That's why he told Hank that he would never draft him in 1987. By their own luck, they inherited him in Cleveland instead. Now they decided Belle needed professional help.

* * *

Albert Jojuan Belle still went by "Joey" when the Indians drafted him as a second-round pick in 1987. Twice named to the All-Southeastern Conference First Team as an outfielder for Louisiana State University, Joey set the Tigers' records in nearly every offensive category. However, his problem was that he heaped mounds of pressure on himself and was prone to outbursts. He had shown signs of rage at LSU, rushing into the stands after hecklers shouted racist remarks at him. Those displays carried into his professional career from the onset.

Rick Wolff needed to find a way to understand the volatile slugger. The two of them went to an early lunch before a game. Belle routinely psyched himself up to play baseball the way he used to on the football field. Two hours before the first pitch, he was already wearing a game face. But at lunch he was pleasant and talkative. It was still early.

Joey Belle was very bright. His athleticism didn't make him an exception to his parents' standards in the classroom. His parents, Albert Sr. and Carrie, were educators who preached the importance of a sound education. Joey was at the top of his graduating class at Huntington High School in Shreveport, Louisiana. He was an Eagle Scout, vice president of his Future Business Leaders of America chapter, and a member of the National Honor Society. But alcohol gave rise to a new side of him; one best characterized by his unfiltered rage. There were days when he would show up to the park surly and hungover. He trashed the clubhouse sink at Triple-A Colorado Springs during a postgame tirade in 1990 after another hitless night, for which the club handed down a five-game suspension.

He gave his mea culpa, but Wolff, like the rest of the Indians staff, still didn't know the root source of Joey's angry outbursts. But soon an answer appeared, an answer that caught many by surprise: Belle was diagnosed by an outside medical expert who insisted that he had issues with alcohol.

Joey spent ten weeks in rehabilitation to treat his alcoholism and went through anger management to lighten his prickly disposition. The clinic's programs encouraged him to reinvent himself. He started the moment he rejoined the Indians in August of 1990, choosing to go only by his given name, Albert, from that point forward.

But even the new-and-improved Albert Belle had Kryptonite. In May of 1991, Albert pelted a fan with a baseball at Municipal Stadium. The fan, Jeff Pillar, had shouted, "Hey, Joey! Keg party at my house after the game!" Belle got a six-game suspension for this episode and was forced to turn over a week's salary to charity. He was going to have to learn to ignore the fan distractions and control his anger if he wanted to stay in the big leagues.[1]

---

[1] Inevitably, Albert had more brush-ups with fans and continued to exhibit destructive behaviors that are discussed again in Chapter Eighteen.

Chapter Eleven

THE 1991 DRAFT: MANNY RAMÍREZ

"There are actually two jobs in baseball with a paper trail for success
in the front office. One's the GM and one's the scouting director.
It's written in blood, and that's essentially what John Hart and I
were faced with."

—Mickey White, former Indians amateur scouting director

Mickey White was forty years old when he took over for Chet Montgomery
to oversee the amateur draft in the United States and the Indians' international focus in Venezuela, Panama, and the Dominican Republic. He had
flown out to Cleveland in September of 1990 to meet with John Hart about
the position while at the time serving as an East Coast cross-checker for the
Seattle Mariners. Mickey and his wife were invited back for a game in Hank
Peters' luxury box, and he got a phone call with the job offer the day after he
returned home. He moved his wife and three kids to Strongsville, a suburb
southwest of Cleveland, in January of 1991 to begin work.

There was a sense of familiarity about Cleveland and its people that hit
home for Mickey, who traces his roots back to Pittsburgh.

"The people were the same, they just wore different colors for the football games," he recalls. "That's how it was when you were dealing with people from the quote-unquote Rust Belt cities. They're all kind of same, very little bulls**t, tell-it-to-your-face kind of people."

He had quite a surprise when he learned his new next-door neighbor had gone to Kent State, where he was a teammate of Steelers great Jack Lambert. The two immediately became friends.

But the change at the head of the scouting department wasn't the only difference for the Indians as the organization prepared for the 1991 amateur draft. Cleveland's back-to-back failures in the first rounds of '89 and '90 prompted Hank Peters to make an announcement when his scouts met at the 1990 Winter Meetings. His decree: Tom Giordano would accompany any scout before signing the club's next No. 1 pick. He didn't want them to mess this next one up, and for good reason. The Indians had been eyeing their eventual top pick for four years, and he was the kind of kid, as scout Joe DeLucca put it, that "you only see once in your life."

***

Joe DeLucca will deny any claim that he *discovered* Manny Ramírez. Everybody knew about Manny when he played ball as a teenager in northern Manhattan's Washington Heights; the same neighborhood that produced Hall of Famer Rod Carew and was the birthplace of Alex Rodriguez. Word got out after the *New York Times* dispatched reporter Sara Rimer, who wrote a series about Manny and his George Washington High School baseball team during his senior year.

DeLucca saw Ramírez for the first time in August of 1988 at the Parade Grounds at Brooklyn's Prospect Park. He had been sent to evaluate a first baseman on a Youth Service League team who was very talented, but rumored to have been living in a nearby crack house. DeLucca went to the park with Eddie Díaz, a former catcher who became a scout after his playing career. Díaz was a strong-looking guy who spoke Spanish and grew up in Washington Heights after leaving the Dominican Republic. He always tagged along with

DeLucca, especially when he ventured into rougher parts of the borough or to scout Hispanic players, and he was particularly helpful on the day he came across Manny on the sandlot at Prospect Park.

When DeLucca arrived at the park, he found the prospect he came to evaluate had a pencil-thin physique, a drawn-out face, and rings around his eyes, confirming the scout's suspicions about the first baseman's connections to drugs. So as to not waste the trip, DeLucca began assessing the talent on the surrounding sandlots. That's when he laid eyes on Manny Ramírez in the batter's box.

Giordano would agree later, upon seeing Manny take batting practice, that he had tremendous bat speed. He commented that Manny swung just about the best bat he had ever seen. That's quite a superlative coming from the same guy who scouted Reggie Jackson and Cal Ripken Jr. This kid was quick, exact, and he was only fifteen! The hitting mechanics needed some adjusting, but that could easily be fixed with instruction. However, Manny's plate appearance that day in the park piqued DeLucca's interest enough that he sent his companion, Díaz, to meet him after he jogged in from center field. DeLucca instructed Díaz to write the boy's phone number and school on the back of a business card; after all, they wanted to have a way to get in touch with him again.

Díaz also grabbed some old batting gloves from the car—a pair he used when he played for one of Cleveland's minor-league affiliates—and presented them to Ramírez in the dugout as a token from their meeting. This gesture drew the attention of Mel Zitter, who ran the YSL program and looked after his players' interests when scouts became involved, and he confronted DeLucca afterward. There would be no scouts luring his kids to sign contracts for a worn set of gloves, and Zitter forbade him from getting close to the players. It was classic Zitter, but it was a trait DeLucca respected: He was the kids' only safety net protecting them from disingenuous scouts looking for bargain signings.

In Zitter's warning, he never told DeLucca that he couldn't try calling Ramírez. After a week, the scout referred to the number on the reverse-side of the business card and waited for the boy to answer on the other end of the line. Only there would be no such luck: Manny didn't give him a working number. The Ramírez family didn't even have a phone in their apartment. Maybe the boy was bashful and gave Díaz arbitrary digits, saving himself from embarrassment. In any case, it wasn't an emergency. DeLucca and a handful of scouts from Cleveland and around the league were always there to watch Manny's every move any time he set foot on a diamond over the course of the next four years.

Associate scouts like Díaz went to see the boy when DeLucca couldn't. DeLucca was responsible for evaluating every prospect from New York to New England, and Manny was always playing ball. Ramírez had five or six games per week, split between his high school and YSL teams, whose game settings were altogether different.

The Spanish-speaking community turned out for George Washington's contests, chanting and cheering from the first pitch through the final out. It reminded DeLucca of the vociferous crowds in Santo Domingo, who rallied for teams like the *Leones* and *Tigres* of the Dominican professional league. Manny was thirteen when he moved from Santo Domingo to New York, so he was familiar with the games' electric feel and all the chatter. It charged him up in the batter's box. He was a three-time All-City selection who hit .650 his senior year, swatting 14 home runs over twenty-two games, en route to being named the Public School Athletic League's (PSAL) Player of the Year.

All the commotion around the high school games would have been a distraction in the field for typical teenage sensations with major-league aspirations. For that reason, DeLucca speculates, Manny's high school manager had him play third base so he could talk to him through the game and keep him focused. The turf and dirt on the public schools' infields weren't exactly pristine, but the conditions didn't take away from Manny's performance. He routinely made clean picks and showed off a plus-arm from the hot corner.

"He really could have been a third baseman," DeLucca notes.

In fact, that's where the Mets worked him out when they evaluated him before the draft . . . but that's not where the Indians envisioned him. The club preferred him in the outfield. That's where DeLucca saw him most, patrolling center field for his YSL teams. He ranked Manny as the top prospect in the region when he sent monthly reports to Mickey White.

George Lauzerique, the Indians' East Coast scout, praised Ramírez, but cautioned Joe DeLucca about tabbing him as a top choice.

"I love this kid, but he ain't ever gonna be a first rounder," DeLucca remembers Lauzerique saying. George Lauzerique was from Cuba and had been in Manny's shoes before, having been drafted by the Kansas City Athletics after a promising career of his own at George Washington High School. Teams didn't roll the dice on Latin-American immigrant kids in the first round in those days, as the U.S. dollar was worth fourteen-times more when converted to Dominican *pesos oros* at the time of Manny's MLB debut in 1993. Because Ramírez was in the country on a green card, who was to say that he wouldn't cash in on his signing bonus and return to his homeland to enjoy his fortune with friends and family? He was also going to be nineteen, and would not finish high school. Was this kid worth the risk?

Mickey White certainly thought he was.

"There's a million reasons not to do something, and only one to do it," he says, looking back at the decision. "I believed Manny was the right guy. There are players out there who play because they are almost obsessive-compulsive about baseball. That's something that resonates clearly at that level of player. I'm still obsessed with baseball; not to the point that I don't eat or sleep, but the passion and curiosity that I have for the sport is still there. If you've got that in your heart and you see that in another player, there's a sentiment that resonates like a string being plucked."

Mickey White and John Hart went to the Big Apple to see Ramírez play again in person, as Cleveland had other viable options it needed to consider for its first selection of the draft. Danny O'Dowd had been lobbying for Aaron Sele, a 6-foot-3-inch right-hander who starred at Washington State University. The front office saw another potential choice in Allen Watson, a southpaw from the New York Institute of Technology in Long Island. John went to see Watson pitch at 10:30 one Sunday morning in Levittown, and then trekked to Prospect Park to watch Ramírez. He saw Manny hit a long drive as soon as he got out of the car, and started raving about his swing on the way to the field.

On the return flight back to Cleveland, Hart asked White what he thought about the players, and the scouting director was just as enamored with the kid from Santo Domingo and his sweet swing. Mickey was ready to sell him on his first pick.

"John, you know I'm from Pittsburgh. I told myself, if I ever had a chance to draft Roberto Clemente, this is the closest thing I've seen to him," White said. There was no disagreement from Hart. Now it was a matter of making an offer, drafting, and signing the kid.

The Indians had failed three times to get in touch with Ramírez to determine his willingness to sign, so DeLucca got a hold of Mel Zitter to act as an intermediary. There had been a time that DeLucca thought Zitter was acting as a bird dog for the Cubs, as that was the speculation around his YSL fields. Bird dogs referred players to teams' regional scouts and occasionally earned kickbacks when those prospects signed. Zitter got that reputation after some of his players (most notably Shawn Dunston and, later, Alex Arias) signed with Chicago. DeLucca would not feel comfortable talking to Manny if he was already being shuffled to the Cubs.

Zitter was receptive to the scout's concern and assured him that it was not the case. After quelling DeLucca's apprehensions, Zitter set up a date for the Indians to meet with Manny to conduct his signability.

The meeting place was a twenty-four-hour diner called George's near Prospect Park. Giordano went with DeLucca per their general manager's request. Zitter insisted on joining them, too, lest the team's representatives try to pull a quick one with his player. The three men chatted in a booth, waiting for Manny to arrive. DeLucca was relieved when he looked out the diner window and saw him hop off the bus across the street.

Manny sat down at the table and DeLucca could tell that he was shy. He ordered a bowl of soup, a hamburger, and a soda, which he scarfed down. The scout tried engaging him with questions about his parents and siblings, school, his girlfriend, and if he really wanted to be a baseball player. Manny didn't look up from the table, nodding and responding with "uh-huhs" between bites. He looked over at Zitter for additional cues, but slowly started to open up, especially after Giordano offered him another round of food. Manny first shook his head no, but Zitter flagged a waitress and ordered him a second helping anyway.

DeLucca interjected after Manny finished eating.

"Now look," he said, "You know why we're here. If we should draft you, would you play for the Cleveland Indians?"

Zitter let him answer.

"Yeah, I like the Indians," Ramírez said. Giordano later asked Zitter what it would take to sign Manny. He needed to give the management in Cleveland an estimate.

Zitter said it depended on what round they were thinking.

"We're talking the first round," Giordano said. DeLucca promised they would be fair to him. They weren't going to cheat him out of the money he was going to be due.

Zitter's jaw dropped as the scene unfolded: He was in disbelief, and it indicated to DeLucca that no other team had contacted him about making Manny their top priority. Only one other team, the Minnesota Twins, projected Manny's name to be called before the fifth round at the earliest.

Zitter had come prepared, armed with a list of signing bonuses awarded to the 1990 draft picks. His demands: The discussion for Manny's services started at $10,000 more than the Indians' first-round pick from the previous year, plus 10 percent. The Indians estimated that would bring the bonus to about $300,000, which was still an unheard-of sum for a mid-first-round high school pick. In comparison, Ken Griffey Jr. only got $160,000 from the Mariners for being the top pick in the '87 draft, but wasn't anywhere near the record-setting $1.5 million the Yankees awarded Brien Taylor, whom they took with the No. 1 pick in 1991. Manny's money would be most comparable to the $275,000 that Larry "Chipper" Jones received when the Atlanta Braves drafted him out of Florida State as the first pick in 1990, and John Hart could have thrown in more cash if DeLucca needed it to sign his prospect.

DeLucca went out to the park to talk to Zitter at YSL's Sunday doubleheader. It was blistering hot for only the first week of June. As if the heat wasn't enough to wear him out, Manny had worked out in front of the Mets for six hours the day before and had blisters on both hands. It didn't stop him from hitting eighteen balls out of the park during batting practice the next day; however, he was dragging by the second game, and it showed.

The Seattle Mariners' leading scout and the assistant to the general manager were on hand and saw a lackluster performance from Manny at the park, marked by a poor showing in the batter's box and an uncharacteristic lack of hustle. Nevertheless, their presence gave DeLucca a tinge of nervousness. Could the M's suddenly be interested in signing his top pick? Seattle was two slots ahead of Cleveland at No. 11. The Mariners' personnel caught up with Zitter along the foul line in right field after the game and chatted for about ten minutes, but when they passed DeLucca on the way to the parking lot, they wished him luck. DeLucca interpreted this to mean that the Mariners were not pursuing Ramírez after all.

The next day, the Indians selected Manny Ramírez with the 13th pick of the 1991 draft. Giordano flew out to New York and met DeLucca for the signing, which took place in the Ramírez' apartment in Washington Heights. Zitter was there, too, and he collected a $10,000 check from the Indians to put toward his YSL programs.

When Giordano returned to Cleveland with the signed contract in tow, the congregation in the office let out a cheer. The Indians finally had their first-round pick.

* * *

The scouting department's successes in the 1991 draft didn't stop with the selection of Manny Ramírez. Cleveland went on to draft Florida Gators third baseman Herbert Perry with their second round pick, and LSU Tigers pitchers Chad Ogea and Paul Byrd heard their named called by the Indians in the third and fourth rounds. All three players were playing in the big leagues by 1995.

In all, the Chet Montgomery and Mickey White eras saw almost fifty players reach the major leagues.

"That's an aberration, in terms of numbers," White says. "If you have that many guys coming from your system at one snapshot, odds are it's a direct indication that you've done a good job scouting."

And it was a good reflection on Hank Peters for his staff's ability to complete one of its principal tasks in his final draft. Hank felt content leaving the Indians with an arsenal of young talent, from which the organization could make call-ups to the majors in the coming seasons or swap as trade bait. He left Cleveland in a much better place than where they had been when he took the reins.

Chapter Twelve

FIRING JOHNNY MAC, INTRODUCING HARGROVE

Hank Peters' dealing of pitchers Tom Candiotti and Bud Black later in June of 1991 left the big-league club deflated. John McNamara didn't have more experienced pitchers to take over their places in the starting rotation, which made it even more difficult for the manager to win ball games. By midsummer, Cleveland was the shameful owner of a 25–52 record (the worst mark in baseball), and Municipal Stadium felt like a pressure cooker. The humid air was sticky and moist, and it felt thick enough to be sliced by Chief Wahoo's hatchet. Even worse, the waves of mayflies emanating from Lake Erie—or Canadian soldiers as they are often called around northeast Ohio—buzzed around heads, hands, and feet, pestering the brave sampling of fans who ventured out to the ballpark. Under the lights, swarms of the little brown waterborne bugs looked like rainfall against the July nighttime sky. But as if the weather and those damn midges hadn't made Hank's staff and the fans stricken and miserable, the Indians' circus antics on the field left them all waiting to be put out of their misery. From June 6 to July 3, the team went an abysmal 3–23, with losing streaks of five (twice), six, and seven games, which included sweeps by Minnesota (twice), Toronto, Detroit, and New York.

And so, two months before Hank Peters was to leave for retirement (and just shy of the season's halfway point), the general manager was again faced with another critical decision about the team's leadership in the dugout. However, it was painfully evident to Hank that this managerial swap would be altogether different from any change he had ever made, as it required him to fire one of his closest friends around baseball: John McNamara.

The firing took place on July 6. It was a Saturday morning, and Peters called a press conference, at which he made his comments on the state of the club. He also made Johnny Mac's dismissal official.

"I think this year, he probably did as well as could be expected under the circumstances," Peters told reporters. "This club is very much dedicated to going with a young team, but it's inexperienced. As a result of this, we have a different club today than the one we had a year ago, and it was my belief it was the type of club John might not be accustomed to managing."

The GM shouldered a portion of the blame as well.

"John McNamara is not a scapegoat," he said rather diplomatically, adding, "He's not totally to blame for what has happened here. If there was a shortage of talent on this ball club in the minds of any of you, that responsibility is on my shoulders and the shoulders of management."

Despite Peters' admission, the effects of his firing were devastating to McNamara, and he would never manage again in the majors following his stint in Cleveland. Worse, it put a strain on his relationship with Peters that lingered longer than either man cared to mention.

McNamara lamented but understood that what needed to be done was done.

"When you're a manager, you don't know any day when that axe could fall."

Even so, it was a necessary move in the organization's progression. Some felt that McNamara's replacement, Mike Hargrove, should have been the club's initial hire instead of Johnny Mac to begin with.

"All along we looked at Mike as being an heir apparent to the manager's position," says Peters.

Broadcasters referred to Mike Hargrove during his playing career as "The Human Rain Delay" for his elaborate pre-pitch routine at the plate. He would step out of the batter's box and smack the barrel of his bat against the bottom of his shoes, reach behind to hike up his pants from the left-hip pocket, readjust his gloves to fit tightly around his hands, readjust the donut he wore on his left thumb, flex his shoulders, touch his helmet and wipe his hands on his pants before either 1) repeating the ritual or 2) stepping back into the box for the next pitch.

Despite that nickname, "Grover" was the name that followed him during his career as a player and into the dugout.

It was actually Hank Peters' predecessor, former club president Dan O'Brien, who kept Hargrove involved with baseball after he retired as a player in 1985. After hanging up his spikes, Hargrove and O'Brien came up with a plan for him to pursue managing.

"I think all of us—people in the stands, my wife, the players on the bench—we all sit there and watch the manager work a ball game and you see him do something, move a player here, change pitchers, put a hit-and-run on or squeeze and the first question is, 'Why is he doing that?' and if it doesn't work out, 'Why doesn't he try something else?'" Hargrove says, so as to justify his initial interests to manage. "What better way to test all of those 'what-ifs' when I played than to go out and try to do it myself?"

Hargrove felt that his best opportunity to begin coaching was going to be with the Indians or the Rangers, after having played in both organizations. He had already put in twelve years of major-league service time between Cleveland and Arlington, highlighted by his distinction as the American League Rookie of the Year in 1974 with Texas and six years as the Indians' everyday first baseman. His first assignment with Cleveland was as a hitting instructor at its Rookie affiliate in Batavia, New York, in 1986, after which he was promoted to manage the Indians' high-A affiliate in the Carolina League, the Kinston Indians, the following year. He got promoted again in 1988 to Double-A Louisville and to Triple-A Colorado Springs in 1989, which is an unusually fast progression for aspiring managers. But the Perryton, Texas, native had professional experience and a disarming personality that endeared him to his players and made for a rapid ascent up the farm ladder.

Hargrove's next promotion was to the big-league club, where he would become the first-base coach under Johnny Mac. It was implied that Hargrove was being groomed for the manager's job in the future. Though Hargrove had been away from the major leagues and had been cutting his teeth as a minor-league manager, Peters thought it would have been best to give him a coaching position on the staff so that he could learn from an experienced manager in the big leagues first. Plenty had changed in the majors since Hargrove had been around, including the attitudes of players and the way that clubs were handling them.

"It gave him the opportunity to get updated with what was going on at the major-league level so that when the time came that I felt the change was necessary, he would be there as the man I felt was well suited," recalled Peters.

Hargrove benefited from being back in the majors, where he could be tutored by Johnny Mac each night at the ballpark. Hargrove was in charge of the defense and watched the manager perform in-game moves, call plays, make player substitutions, and handle the press.

"I didn't really think along those lines," Hargrove says about working with the media. "You talk to them before the game and after the game, they have the demands on your time as a manager that you never really had as a player or even as a minor-league manager."

When the Indians returned from the All-Star break in 1991 with Hargrove as the new manager, he was still making the adjustment. He had always liked to accommodate writers who approached him as a player in the clubhouse, but he soon realized he couldn't manage the ball club efficiently and maintain all of the same practices.

"I always felt like I was playing catch-up. I didn't realize that I had to prioritize and set schedules with [public relations], and so that was difficult to get used to," he says.

It was a critical lesson for Hargrove to grasp early on in his managing career because he would surely have to cater to more media requests and balance his schedule more effectively as his team grew in prominence.

Chapter Thirteen

HART'S DEALS AND
THE FIVE-YEAR PLAN

Helping turn around a professional franchise felt more exhausting than John Hart's days playing baseball. It zapped more of his energy and was more physically demanding than when he was teaching and coaching in a public high school, plus the job seemed just as thankless. As his team staggered out of ballparks at 1 and 2 a.m. after getting swept by the likes of the Yankees, Blue Jays, and Red Sox, Hart couldn't help but wonder when the Indians would start to see the light at the end of the tunnel.

"Those five years the Indians spent restructuring the organization through 1994 were the hardest I could remember working," Hart says.

Yet there was a clear indication that the franchise had taken steps toward realizing Dick Jacobs' vision when it was time for Hank Peters to finally pass the torch to Hart at the end of the 1991 season.[1] Another phase of the Indians' return to being a competitive team was just taking shape.

---

[1] Peters had pieced together the front office that would carry the Indians to success in the future. Notably, one of Peters' final personnel moves before retirement was the hiring of Mark Shapiro, the son of Baltimore attorney and sports agent Ron

John Hart outlined what he called the "five-year plan" with Dan O'Dowd and manager Mike Hargrove to map the club's deal strategy, which would continue the Indians' transformation toward becoming a contender. In this five-year plan, there were four key components: the draft, smart trades, long-term contracts for prime players, and select free-agent signings, when appropriate, to put the team in a playoff position. Some aspects of the plan had already been initiated during Peters' tenure. For example, the draft hauls in 1989 and 1991 provided them depth in the farm system to develop talent for the major-league club or for trade purposes.

Hank Peters had also made the first of many smart trades during this era to secure additional young talent for their roster of the future; having swapped Joe Carter with San Diego for Sandy Alomar Jr. and Carlos Baerga. By 1991, the impact of that deal would become plainly visible: Alomar made his second of three consecutive appearances at the All-Star Game, and Baerga made his first of a pair of trips to the midsummer classic. Incidentally, the two players were teammates with Joe Carter on the AL squad at the '92 All-Star Game, after the Padres dealt Carter to the Blue Jays. That goes to show you that Hank went ahead and got two future All-Stars for the price of one. The front office felt that way all along, starting back when the Indians made the deal in the first place, and it had led Giordano to establish his own doctrine for approaching trades. "Whenever you make a deal," Giordano said, "if you want filet mignon, you need to give filet mignon back." He would continue, saying, "You can't give the other guy chuck steak or ground beef and expect filet mignon in return."

Hart took the same approach when he sat at the trading desk in his first winter as general manager in 1991. He sent catcher Eddie Taubensee and

---

Shapiro. The young Mark caught Peters' attention because he was a tech expert at a time when computerization of scouting information and business material was the up-and-coming trend around the league. The front office would use those innovations and continue to grow the club from the farm. Shapiro went on to become the general manager after Hart's tenure in the position.

right-handed pitcher Willie Blair to Houston on December 10 for infielder Dave Rohde and rookie outfielder Kenny Lofton. At the time, it seemed like the kind of deal that would make scouting director Mickey White want to jump from the top of the Terminal Tower. Mickey had taken a strong liking to Taubensee—everyone else in the front office liked him, too. But White thought Taubensee could one day become a Hall of Fame catcher, which is why he didn't want to see him traded.

"We really didn't have anybody else behind Sandy with an elevated profile," White says, defending his reasons for wishing to hang on to Taubensee.

Cleveland had picked up Taubensee off waivers from Oakland in April of '91, after White badgered Peters and Hart. At first, White had only managed to get an "I'll think about it" out of Peters, and he bugged Hart about claiming Taubensee one night at dinner.

"I don't want to be a pain in the ass about this, John," Mickey said.

"You are being a pain in the ass about this," John shot back. "If you really want to take him and you want to put your job on the line, we'll take him," John said. Mickey persisted and Cleveland acquired Taubensee.

Hart recalled White's persistence, and he went right back to him when he evaluated the trade possibility at the winter meetings after the season. In fact, it took Hart by surprise when White told him he stayed up all night thinking about the Houston trade and instructed him to, "Make the f***ing deal!"

"How can you be so strong on one side and today be on the other?" Hart asked. White didn't really want to see Taubensee go, but his trade value could better serve the Indians in the long run if it meant bringing over Kenny Lofton from the Astros. Cleveland was in dire need of a leadoff man who could play center field, and Houston needed a serviceable catcher. The trade could benefit each club on both ends.

White answered, "Yesterday we were just talking about it. Today we make the decision."

And what a decision it was. The trade turned out to be much more favorable for the Indians, to the point that Indians beat writer Paul Hoynes still cracks jokes about there being a warrant for John Hart's arrest for grand larceny in Houston after stealing Lofton. Hoynes' column in the *Plain Dealer* called it the second-best trade in Cleveland history (after the Carter deal), despite the fact that Dave Rohde, the infielder included in the Astros' side of the trade, only played five games in an Indians uniform before suddenly deciding to retire. Taubensee spent two years in Houston and became a mainstay in the Cincinnati Reds' lineup from 1994 through the rest of the decade. Even then, he didn't ever rise to the lofty expectations White set for him when he broke into the big leagues as a twenty-two-year-old.

Kenny Lofton, in return, became the prototypical leadoff man: a lynchpin-type guy for the team who set the table with explosiveness from the first pitch each night. Lofton was a point guard at the University of Arizona, where he ran his Wildcats all the way to the Final Four in 1988.[2] Now his ability to run down baseballs in the alleyways of left- and right-center field made everyone scratch their heads in wonderment.

"He could beat you every way imaginable," says Indians broadcaster Tom Hamilton. "He's the one guy who could draw a walk and end up scoring a run in the very first inning without the benefit of a hit. He manufactured runs. He made catches nobody else could make, and he brought energy and excitement to the ball club that nobody else could do."

Hart's dealing before the 1992 season didn't stop there. He added surehanded first baseman Paul Sorrento during spring training, acquiring him from the Twins for pitchers Curt Leskanic and Oscar Muñoz. Sorrento was another major-league addition, and would be the starting first baseman for the next four seasons in Cleveland.

---

[2] Lofton didn't join the baseball team at the University of Arizona until his junior year. He's one of two people to have played in a Final Four and the World Series. The other is former right-handed pitcher Tim Stoddard, who, curiously enough, also comes from Lofton's hometown of East Chicago, Indiana. Stoddard is the only man to win the NCAA basketball tournament (he won at North Carolina State University during the 1973–1974 season) and the World Series (he was a member of the 1983 Baltimore Orioles).

Chapter Fourteen

BREAKING GROUND

Just as the front office was putting the pieces in place to help the Indians on the field, the owners were doing their part to build them a new one. This had been a chief goal of Dick Jacobs ever since he first approached Pat O'Neill about purchasing the franchise from the estate of his late uncle. Getting the Indians a new stadium was vital to the economic viability of the franchise. After all, they were tenants to the Cleveland Browns, whose owner, Art Modell, and Stadium Corporation, the business he formed to manage Municipal Stadium, restricted the Indians franchise as a whole.

Dick Jacobs once told Terry Pluto at the *Plain Dealer*, "It's hard for two guys to share the same lunchbox."

That was mostly in part due to Modell, who would not share revenues from baseball suites; plus the Indians' ticket sales were sparse. They managed to draw a little more than 655,000 fans in 1985, the league's worst attendance figure for a third consecutive season. Fans could walk up to the box office minutes before the first pitch and buy tickets for the cost of peanuts. Opposing teams grimaced when they came to Cleveland. There was not enough revenue at the gate to make them any money.

Year	Indians Attendance/ Game	Indians Attendance/ Season	League Average/ Season	League Rank (1–26)
1977	11,185	900,365	1,402,825	23
1978	10,070	800,584	1,466,426	24
1979	12,567	1,011,644	1,597,999	22
1980	12,923	1,033,827	1,563,575	23
1981	12,843	661,395	1,004,713	19
1982	12,889	1,044,021	1,648,604	24
1983	9,493	768,941	1,713,647	26
1984	9,007	734,079	1,711,531	26
1985	8,089	655,181	1,752,302	26
1986	18,059	1,471,805	1,798,052	18
1987	13,307	1,077,898	1,948,382	26
1988	17,427	1,411,610	2,035,688	22

What was worse was the stipulation in the Indians' lease agreement, which limited their share of revenue from the scoreboard signage. The Browns allotted the baseball team a reduced cut of $50,000 from the advertising space because the landlord, Art Modell, was the one who sold it. Whether Modell made $5 million or only a dollar, the Indians' return would stay the same.

"We could only generate $50,000 out of the scoreboard of a Major League Baseball team? That's why Dick Jacobs had to get out of there and get into our own building, where we could get some economic viability to create a foundation for this franchise," says Bob DiBiasio, the Indians' senior vice president of public affairs.

There had been a number of failed attempts to build a new baseball stadium prior to the Jacobs brothers' purchase of the Indians. The first of the failed plans called for the construction of a multipurpose sports complex under a dome, which was to be shared by the Indians and Cavaliers, the city's basketball franchise. Public officers had been rallying to bring back basketball to the downtown area, as the Cavs had moved about a half-hour south to the Richfield Coliseum in 1974. The plans for the Greater Cleveland Dome Stadium Corporation's proposal for a $150 million facility was voted down in May of 1984, three years before the Jacobs brothers ever got involved with the Tribe. Cuyahoga County then looked into a second plan called "the Hexatron," a six-sided facility with a retractable roof, which would be funded by a proposed "sin tax" on alcohol and cigarettes. Those plans failed as well.

Keep in mind, of course, that all this came following one of Cleveland's most tumultuous eras. The city had remained the butt of frequent jokes on the late-night talk show circuit for all of its misfortune: A mixture of oils and pollutants on the surface of the Cuyahoga River ignited in 1969, setting the waterway ablaze. Then, Mayor Ralph Perk accidentally lit his hair on fire with a welder's torch at a ribbon-cutting ceremony in 1972, and that nobody tried to extinguish the flames in the mayor's hair with water from the river became the next joke. Northeast Ohio was ravaged by blizzards in the winters of 1977 and 1978, the latter of which even took the name "the Cleveland Superbomb" in meteorological circles because it was the most extreme non-tropical low-pressure system in the recorded history of the continental United States. That same year, during the administration of Mayor Dennis Kucinich, Cleveland defaulted on $15.5 million in loans from Ohio banks, becoming the first American city since the Great Depression to fail to pay off its own financial obligations. The final parting shot in the seventies was that Cleveland's steady population decline allowed it to fall out of the top-ten largest cities in the country.

When George Voinovich was elected as mayor in 1979, he aimed to reinvent Cleveland as the "Comeback City." He managed to bring President Jimmy Carter and candidate Ronald Reagan to town for a presidential debate in 1980. The *Plain Dealer* spearheaded a newspaper campaign in 1981 with a bumper sticker proclaiming, "New York's the Big Apple, but Cleveland's a Plum!" The mayor even threw out the ceremonial first *plum* at a game between the Indians and the Yankees that year. (Rumor has it that the plump, purple fruit splattered in the catcher's mitt.)

Voinovich's tenure in office was marked by unprecedented cooperation from George Forbes and the all-Democrat City Council to bolster economic development and urban revitalization downtown.[1] Among the businessmen leading the efforts to redevelop the downtown area, the Jacobs brothers were at the front of the line. By 1987, they had turned the barren plaza in front of the Erieview Tower into the glass-enclosed Galleria shopping mall, adding seventy stores and a large food court. The following year, they broke ground on the Society Center (now the Key Tower), which would become the tallest building in Cleveland.

"The climate was there for risk taking, and my family decided to take some risks on the hometown," says Jeffrey P. Jacobs, son of former Indians owner Dick Jacobs.

Jeff Jacobs was a Republican representative in the eighties and had spent a year working with Voinovich after his election. Jeff introduced his father to the mayor and to City Council President Forbes, both of whom were impressed by the Jacobs brothers' vision and supportive of their projects.

"The things on the Flats, Erieview, Key Bank Tower . . . those just happened to be the same public-private partnership that would push Gateway forward," Jeff Jacobs recounts.

"Gateway" was the proposed Gateway Sports and Entertainment Complex the brothers wanted to see built along the southern edge of downtown. The project would place the Indians and Cavaliers in side-by-side stadiums, which were to be separated by a spacious plaza and two parking garages. Cleveland Tomorrow, an association of top executives from the city's most influential firms, was committed to making Gateway a reality. The group joined forces with attorney Tom Chema and a new set of civic leaders, including Voinovich and Forbes' successors, Mayor Michael R. White and Cleveland City Council President Jay Westbrook.[2] Their aim was to get the sin tax from the earlier "Hexatron"

---

[1] They put together a plan for tax incremental financing to redirect a 75-percent cut of property taxes from prime, downtown real estate to fund later projects like the construction of the Rock and Roll Hall of Fame and Museum.

[2] Voinovich left his office and became the sixty-fifth governor of Ohio. Forbes lost the race for mayor and returned to private practice as an attorney, before becoming president of the Cleveland NAACP.

proposal back on the ballot during the countywide primary in May of 1990 to publicly finance a portion of the project.[3] White, Westbrook, and Cuyahoga County commissioners Tim Hagan, Virgil Brown, Mary Boyle, and Jim Petro devised a plan for a fifteen-year tax, which tacked $0.019 on the price of beer, $0.015 on liquor, and $0.045 on cigarettes. Ballot Issue 2 was heavily contested. Days before the election, baseball commissioner Fay Vincent attended a city council finance-committee meeting, during which he insinuated that the Indians could one day be forced to leave Cleveland for good if the Gateway proposal was defeated on the ballot. "Should the vote be a negative one, we may find ourselves confronting a subject we want to avoid," Vincent said.

Election Day fell on May 8, and 49.6 percent of registered voters took to the polls. At the conclusion of the voting, Issue 2 was able to pass by a narrow 51.7 percent margin (198,390 votes for, 185,209 votes against). Gateway was going to happen after all, and the Cleveland Indians were finally getting out of Municipal Stadium and into their own building.

However, the tax referendum would only fund $84 million (48 percent) of the cost for a new baseball stadium. The Jacobs brothers would have to come up with the remaining $91 million to fund the "Cleveland Indians Baseball Park."

That's when Dick and David could rely on their business savvy to persuade local businesspeople that they were buying into a civic investment to make it possible. They sought commitments for luxury boxes and advertising in ways they could have never done while at Municipal Stadium.

"They weren't just necessarily buying or leasing a suite to watch a baseball game," DiBiasio said of the area involvement. "The local companies stood up and said, 'Yeah, we believe in this. We believe that Major League Baseball in our town is important. It will create economic impact, and it is something we have to have.'"

In return, Dick Jacobs wanted to see that his new stadium was done right. He helped in the selection of Cleveland-based Osborn Engineering,

---

[3] The tax, which had been suggested by Representative Jeff Jacobs before his father ever bought into the Indians.

which drew up the plans. Osborn was the same firm that did the blueprints for the original Yankee Stadium, Fenway Park, and more than one hundred other major sporting facilities. Dick also helped choose the architectural firm. The Indians contracted HOK Sport from St. Louis, the cutting-edge architects in stadium design at the time.[4] The design firm was just finishing Baltimore's Oriole Park at Camden Yards, the first retro-classic ballpark of the nineties. Oriole Park featured the traditional, asymmetrical fences of varying heights. The interior and exterior design elements incorporated brick, stone, and green paint-finished exposed steel, which reflected the aesthetics of the warehouses of the neighboring industrial district around the ballpark. Dick visited Oriole Park and was confident that HOK would design for him a first-class retro-modern park, a crossover between the traditional field layout and modern exterior elements, which would be viewed as a local masterpiece.

The stadium groundbreaking took place in January of 1992, and by May of that year, the concrete was already being poured. The following month, the Indians invited Mel Harder, the pitcher who started the opening game at Municipal Stadium in 1932, as well as current players Charles Nagy and Sandy Alomar Jr., to throw ceremonial first pitches at the construction site before the crews began work on the new ballpark.

David Jacobs, who had been on the construction side of the Jacobs brothers' development business, watched the progress each week from an old, nearby storage building. He took great pride in watching the cranes piece together the new home for his beloved ball club, and walked the property every Saturday with his nephew, Jeff. But David Jacobs never saw its completion. He fell ill with a case of pneumonia and was taken to the hospital about 3 a.m. on September 17, 1992, where he died later that morning. He was seventy-one years old.

---

[4] HOK Sport became Populous after a management buyout in 2009. It is one of the largest architectural design firms in the world.

Chapter Fifteen

MINOR LEAGUE DEVELOPMENT

With construction of the Indians' future ballpark under way, Dick Jacobs could again check off another box on his to-do list toward reviving the franchise. But that wasn't the only area where the owner was seeing progress. An assessment of the Indians' minor-league affiliates found the organization's operations on the farm going according to plan. By this time, Cleveland had entered enough quality prospects into its farm system to suggest the future of the big-league club was plenty promising. However, the future All-Stars coming through the organization at that time would eventually owe much of their careers' successes to the work they put in with their coaches during those developmental years.

The player development process is by no means seamless, especially in the lower ranks of minor league baseball, and there's much trial and error once the club gets its hands on new talent in camp for the first time. It's not unusual for a player to move from the position he's most accustomed to playing to one the club thinks would make for a better fit. Other players are coaxed into changing the hitting, fielding, or throwing mechanics they have relied on to sign their first professional contracts. The "walk before you run" approach on training fields can make player development seem like raising kids, but, in effect, that's what clubs are doing. They're taking kids and turning them into major leaguers, and that requires the staff to be patient enough to remember what the kids are going through in their first camps.

The vast majority of the players are living away from home on their own for the first time in their young adult lives. Most, if not all, will struggle and endure more bouts of failure than they have ever experienced around the diamond. They'll train tirelessly each morning and sit through endless bus rides to and from mostly empty minor-league ballparks, where they will have to motivate themselves to grind out a performance worthy of a promotion to the next level. It's the type of grind that tries on the body and the spirit, one that even had Manny Ramírez crying the homesick blues to his manager, Dave Keller, at rookie ball.

Manny spent a sizeable chunk of his $850 monthly salary calling home to Washington Heights from the payphone at a Circle-K gas station in Burlington, North Carolina. He found some solace in being able to chat with Keller, who spoke good Spanish, and some of his Dominican-born teammates. Among them was pitcher Julián Tavárez, who was leading the Appalachian League in shutouts in his first professional season in the United States.

* * *

If there was one coach who would be most directly responsible for the Indians' advanced offensive capabilities in the 1990s, it would be Charlie Manuel.

As a player, Manuel loved to hit so much that he'd routinely take swings for as many as two hours a day without stopping as part of his batting practice regimen. His hitting earned him the nickname "The Red Devil" during a six-year stint in Japan at the end of his playing career, and "The Grinder" back stateside. Even then, Charlie couldn't stop his hitting after his career took him off the field and into the dugout, and hit more than some of his players when he coached in the Minnesota Twins organization in the mid-eighties.

Giordano once saw Manuel's players circled around to watch as their manager hit one towering blast after another, drawing *oohs* and *ahhs* from everyone standing around the cage. When he was finished, Manuel wandered out behind an L-screen and began throwing batting practice. He shocked colleagues when they learned he threw all regular batting practice and extra sessions in the minors up through the time he became a big-league hitting coach. That totaled as many as four hours per day of throwing.

"I didn't like telling people that," Manuel confesses. "Twenty minutes now is considered a day's work."

Manuel didn't shy away from the commitment to hitting. He always wanted to coach the best hitting team in the league. When he joined Mike Hargrove's staff in Cleveland, "Grover" would needle him, saying: "The only thing you wanna see us do is hit. I'm the head coach, I want us to be the best, period." To which Manuel would counter: "We'll win a lot of games if we hit well!"

And Manuel was right. The ball club would eventually win because of its ability to dominate in the batter's box, but that all resulted from the routine he designed for his players. His instruction was centered upon repetition for muscle memory and specific detail to address individual players' habits at the plate. Charlie saw to it that each of his players had a personalized matchup sheet waiting on the chairs at their lockers and video logs for the pitchers they would be facing when they showed up at the ballpark. If they didn't like it, they could always ball it up and throw it away. (Nobody ever did, as they wouldn't dare going against the wishes of the Grinder.)

Before heading onto the field for pregame exercises, Manuel had players shuffling in and out of batting cages, where the work involved soft toss into nets, 25 to 50 cuts, discussion about the opposing team's pitching staff, and what he wanted the lineup to accomplish that game. Manny and other players cycled through 15- and 20-minute sessions. Manny, in particular, liked to see a bevy of breaking balls. He had a tremendous work ethic and a very natural approach, but hitting those pitches didn't come naturally.

"I remember getting reports from rookie ball and it seemed like he hit a home run every night," Manuel recalls, "but he was very dedicated."

Following his "warm-ups," the team took swings for about an hour and a half on the field. Charlie never stood behind the cage; he preferred to throw batting because he mimicked pitchers' motions on the mound. He would dig into the mound with his foot, like he was trying to hold on a runner, and challenged hitters with sinkers, breaking balls, and cutters. He even simulated release points, going over the top or three-quarters to be as similar to the pitchers the team was due to face that day.

Unlike most of the players who just took batting practice, Jim Thome was more into live hitting on the field with Manuel. He would routinely spend 30 to 40 minutes working in the batting cage, but liked to get extra swings in the actual competitive setting. The thinking with Jim as far as hitting was concerned was different, Manuel noted. Thome had an inside-out swing at the start of his professional career that made the left-hander more prone to hit to left field. Manuel didn't want to take his power away, so he moved him closer to the plate, effectively making pitches across the outside corner look like they were dialed down the middle.

"It's how we taught him to pull the ball," Manuel says.

For instance, Manuel challenged him one year at spring training. He and Thome got onto the field to start work, and it was known that he liked to take a lot of pitches, especially with runners in scoring position. Manuel instead told him to expand his strike zone in those situations, but reminded him not to swing at bad pitches out of the zone. He forced Thome to determine which pitches were balls and strikes as they came out of the pitcher's hand. He consistently hit good balls as long as they were strikes. So as they stood there on the field, Manuel offered a dare.

"Hit a homer into those palm trees in right, and dinner's on me," he called out.

John McNamara had been standing nearby to attest. Thome laughed. He was still growing into his burly frame then, but he saw a pitch he liked and offered up a mighty hack, sending the baseball clear over a pair of palm trees sprouting up from behind the fence.

"Well, Jimmy," Manuel started, "Looks like I owe you dinner then." He gave a self-effacing laugh and headed off to the clubhouse. Manuel used those types of tactics to motivate players to work and improve as they progressed to the big leagues. It wasn't long before Thome launched his first major-league homer, a two-run shot against Steve Farr at Yankee Stadium on October 4, 1991. Joel Skinner handed him his bat, a Louisville Slugger T141 model with a clear finish, and told him: "Hey kid, you're gonna get a fastball. Don't miss it." Thome's blast skyrocketed into the upper deck high above right field and put the Indians ahead to a 3–2 victory over the Bronx Bombers. Similarly, Manuel turned to other players around the clubhouse to push younger hitters and they developed. He often used Albert Belle as an example because he was the most intense in the cage and on the field.

"The other guys wanted to keep up with him," Manuel said.

He'd walk about the clubhouse bragging about Belle's hitting. As a result, the younger players wanted to out-hit him. Manuel did that sort of thing as he moved up in the organization with the club's prized hitting prospects.

By the time he took over as the big-league hitting coach in 1994, he had already worked with most, if not every player, in the batting order enough to know their tendencies and how to best assist them.

As a supplement to the work in the cage, Rick Wolff offered mental batting practice for the club's young prospects. Take Manny Ramírez, for example. He had trouble dealing with 0-for-3 nights early on in Burlington (rookie ball), and it was beginning to frustrate him. He looked at his batting average every day, grimacing whenever his numbers dropped.

Wolff had a tactic to simplify his mental approach. He pulled him aside in the outfield one day and posed a question.

"You can get ten hits in thirty at-bats, right?" he asked.

Manny nodded and replied, "Yeah, that's easy."

"That's all it takes to be a .300 hitter, then," Rick said.

And it clicked. Instead of worrying on the nights he didn't collect two or three hits, Ramírez took a step back and began to review his performance over a larger span of plate appearances.

Wolff also incorporated personalized cue cards to help other players along with their approach. He had a discussion with Jim Thome, who was still developing in the minors, and asked him about where his mind was the moment he stepped into the batter's box. What did he look for? The pitcher's face? The little "box" over his shoulder, where he could see the ball at its release point? Thome's approach was even simpler than that.

He had already started pointing his bat like Roy Hobbs (Robert Redford) from the movie *The Natural* to relax the muscles in his arm. He learned to clear his head at the plate, and that all he needed to think about was mentally identifying, "Good pitch, bad pitch," which he took from his work with Manuel. So that's what went on his cue cards.

Wolff's influence didn't stop with the players. He rounded up the coaching staff and personnel to help with their holistic approach as they dealt with players. He made the coaches evaluate the way they addressed their teams and encouraged them to change as they felt necessary.

Mike Hargrove was comfortable having Rick Wolff around on his staff. Rick was familiar with the skipper as a competitor, as the two had become acquainted in 1973, when they played low A-ball in the Western Carolina League. Hargrove was a first baseman with the Gastonia Rangers, who faced Rick and the Tigers' affiliate from Anderson, South Carolina, more than fifteen times that season.

Wolff opened the staff's eyes to some of the unseen cultural biases in dealing with players. The coaches came to expect specific behaviors from American-born players in given situations, and others from Latin American players, many of whom didn't speak much English. The groups of players often responded differently, which puzzled their instructors. Some coaches thought they were being difficult or lazy. That might have been all they knew or how they were taught to respond, Wolff explained. "These kids didn't grow up in Orange County."

* * *

The trickle-down effect of the organization's changed approach was remarkable. The Indians' Triple-A affiliate, the Colorado Springs Sky Sox, was crowned as the '92 champion of the Pacific Coast League. The parent club could probably have seen that coming; the Sky Sox had already clinched four straight playoff berths before taking the league title and was feeding players into the majors. Cleveland's high-A affiliate, the Kinston Indians, had won the Carolina League in 1988 and 1991. Brawny slugger Albert Belle and pitcher Steve Olin helped the K-Tribe to the '88 title, and were called up to the big leagues not long thereafter. Other notable prospects on the '91 squad included Brian Giles, Paul Byrd, Curt Leskanic, and Robert Person.

The player development program was not far from propelling the Tribe into position to become a contender, and the rest of Major League Baseball was starting to take notice. After the '92 season, the Indians received special distinction as the organization of the year, a title handed down by *Baseball America* at the magazine's annual awards banquet. It was a good omen for the direction in which the franchise was heading after John Hart's first full campaign as general manager, but the honor was more of a testament to the efforts of Hank Peters' scouting department and Danny O'Dowd overseeing player development.

Chapter Sixteen

GREG SWINDELL AND
THE LONG-TERM DEAL

After taking over the Indians, Dick Jacobs had to fork over a sum of $10 million as part of the Major League Baseball owners' collusion settlement with the MLBPA (Player's Association). It had been found out that league owners were to have cheated free agents out of $280 million from 1985 to 1987, just as the Jacobs brothers were acquiring their stake in the franchise. Collusion was generally interpreted as a "gentleman's agreement" among the owners to not sign each other's players, effectively driving down the value of their salaries. The MLB Collective Bargaining Agreement protected against the practice, stating, "Players shall not act in concert with other Players and Clubs shall not act in concert with other Clubs."

During the first sequence of owner collusion in 1985, only four out of thirty-five free agents on the market signed with new teams, and that was because their old organizations no longer wanted them. The free agents who went unsigned included household names like the Tigers' Kirk Gibson, the Angels' Tommy John, and the Yankees' Phil Niekro, who weren't tendered new contracts. The Indians were found to have owed back pay to eight players from 1986 and fourteen players from 1987.

At the time of the settlement, Dick made the comment to John Hart, "That's an expensive hot dog I just bought." So just imagine how they felt when they were told they had to pay Greg Swindell $2.02 million after arbitration in 1991!

Arbitration is one of any general manager's least favorite words in the entire baseball lexicon—especially when his club is on the wrong side of the decision in the case, at which point it can be deemed an eleven-letter curse word. The collective bargaining agreement lays out a slew of rules and regulations to spell out a player's arbitration eligibility. Among them: having less than six years of MLB service and not being able to agree with his team on a new contract by the prescribed deadline.

Players typically make the base salary for their first two to three years of service in the majors, and because they have little to no leverage in negotiating for their contracts, they turn to arbitration, as it gives them an opportunity to plead their cases for better compensation with a mediator and their clubs present. The best part (or worst, depending on the side you're on) is that the arbitrator's decision is binding, so the club then has to abide by it and pay up.

For that reason, players and their respective clubs will go to great lengths for the more warm and fuzzy approach; that is, to settle before the contract deadline and avoid the more uncomfortable route in the courtroom. But should both parties remain at odds after the deadline has passed and elect to pursue the latter option, the player and team representatives appear before a three-person MLB labor relations panel in February and, in a best-case scenario, conduct an orderly discussion to work through the contract dispute. More often, arbitration consists of the team's hour-long presentation on why the player isn't worth as much as he claims to be, the player's hour of self-defense, and a half-hour allocation for each party to issue rebuttals and summarize its argument. Team representatives have to downplay or even criticize the quality of the player's contribution to the team on and off the field, including an assessment of his public appeal. They compare the player to his counterparts and equivalents around the league if he is of "special quality." Comments are also made on his physical and mental attributes, taking time to highlight any defects that would take away from his contractual value to the ball club. It can be a dehumanizing process; more like inspecting a thoroughbred before its purchase than negotiating a contract. Feelings can get hurt (and often are).

Enter Greg Swindell, Cleveland's first-round pick in 1986 and the last player to beat the Indians in arbitration. Swindell was a former standout pitcher at the University of Texas, and made $60,000 in his first season of pro ball. His salary the following year increased to $68,750, but Swindell experienced a sophomore slump and saw his record slide to 3–8. When Swindell disputed his contract for 1988, the arbitrators sided with the Indians and awarded him $90,000 instead of the $110,000 he requested. Swindell took that disappointment with him to the field that year as motivation and won a career-best 18 games, going the distance 12 times. He got off to an even better start in 1989, was named to the All-Star Game, and had been leading all left-handers in the American League with 13 wins by August, when his ailing elbow sent him to the disabled list. Upon returning from the DL, Swindell posted an 0–3 mark over his last seven starts, closing out the season with a 13–6 record. This cost him $50,000 in his salary dispute before the 1990 season. However, it was Swindell who had the last laugh when he and the Indians went to arbitration in February of 1991, unsatisfied with the club's initial offer of $1.4 million. The arbitrators sided with Swindell, who, at twenty-six, was about to receive the biggest payday to-date in his six-year career: $2,025,000.

"When we left the room, we thought it was a hard-fought contest but we felt we won, not decisively but by a margin enough to make us feel comfortable," said Swindell's agent, Randy Hendricks, to reporters. They should have felt plenty comfortable. In winning the case, Hendricks' client and his new salary suddenly landed him in the top 10 percent with the league's highest-paid pitchers. If it wasn't bad enough that the Indians had to fork over almost $700,000 more than the club's proposed offer, the fact that Swindell was saddled with his worst record as a starter should have been enough to convince John Hart to never again go to arbitration with a player. (Swindell's major-league best ratio of 5.45 strikeouts per walk couldn't make up for his 9–16 record.)

Elsewhere around baseball, Hart saw the effects of arbitration working against the Pittsburgh Pirates, who had a similar situation with being in a smaller-sized market. The Bucs claimed three straight titles in the National League East, but the team's core of young stars quarreled with the organization over their contracts. Their asking prices would be too high for the Pirates to retain them when they became free agents, and their departure in favor of more lucrative deals dealt the club a crippling blow that haunted the team for almost twenty years.

The first to go was Bobby Bonilla, who made four consecutive trips to the midsummer classic between 1988 and 1991. Going into the '91 season, he lost his arbitration bid for $3.47 million, instead earning $2.4 million in his final season in the Steel City. He opted for the Mets' offer of five years and $29 million when he became a free agent in 1992, leaving Barry Bonds and Andy Van Slyke behind in the Pirates' outfield.

Bonds hit .301, powered 33 homers, and drove in 114 runs en route to collecting his first MVP award in 1990, but even he was denied his arbitration bid for $3.3 million and instead made $2.3 million for the 1991 season. After the negotiations for a long-term deal slowed, Bonds told the organization he wanted to be traded and that it would someday come back and haunt them. It's safe to say that it did. Barry signed with the San Francisco Giants after another MVP season in Pittsburgh in 1992. There was no way he could refuse the offer he received from the Giants' general manager, Bob Quinn: six years, $43.75 million, making Bonds the highest-paid player in history at the time. (Bonds also went on to win the MVP award five more times by the Bay.)

Doug Drabek, a former Cy Young Award winner, also departed Pittsburgh after the 1992 season, accepting a deal from the Houston Astros to return to his native Texas. Having experienced the disappointment of arbitration once with Swindell and witnessing the onset of the Pirates' demise, John Hart sought a method to circumvent the process altogether. Cleveland didn't have a real market advantage over Pittsburgh and would be in the same situation with its prospects one day if he didn't do something to avoid it. He even complained to Danny O'Dowd, stating that "The arbitrator is not even a baseball guy. We're never going to go through this again."

That's when the duo shared a forehead-slapping revelation. The answer they came up with was to sign the Indians' budding stars to long-term contracts while they could still afford them. The strategy relied on a study that showed an inverse correlation between a team's winning percentage and whether it spent more than 17 percent of its payroll on a single player. Hart and O'Dowd used it as their competitive edge to stay ahead of the rapid salary inflation that took place over the nineties. The value of the strategy was three-fold:

1. Not a single superstar would dominate the Indians' payroll.
2. A player became easier to keep if he performed well or easier to deal if necessary (based on the franchise's financial commitment to the player).
3. The Indians could spend what they felt was appropriate to retain the player while they still had his rights, instead of letting the market dictate his price as a free agent.

John Hart assumed a substantial risk in taking this aggressive approach on signing players. He was really sticking out his neck on this one. He hadn't even been a major-league general manager for a full year, yet here he was, asking Dick Jacobs to write millions of dollars in checks for a plan that had never before been carried out. Executives from other clubs were sure to raise their eyebrows at him. Some general managers from competing teams even called him asking why he would dare to take such a chance with unproven talent with the welfare of his club hanging in the balance. Oh, the retribution to be had if this epiphany turned into nothing more than a folly.

John Hart and Dan O'Dowd pitched the concept to Mr. Jacobs, who thought it was a groundbreaking idea.

Dick Jacobs was never averse to taking risks, and as he was in the process of getting his new stadium, he needed his general manager to channel the interest of the Indians' fan base around the club with a team identity the franchise could retain for years to come.

"It was always us spinning guys off when they got to their fourth or fifth years before they became free agents, and we'd have to send them away in order to get more players," Hart says. "This was us really making a stand and Dick was supportive of it."

The owner ascribed to the idea and opened his checkbook.

Hart and O'Dowd finalized twelve multiyear contracts that winter before the 1993 season, and six more the following year to lock up talent and ensure the Indians' most valued players stayed in town.

The Indians awarded the first of the significant extensions to Sandy Alomar Jr., despite the fact that he missed almost half of the 1992 season after surgery to repair torn cartilage in his left knee. Sandy was the 1990 AL Rookie of the Year, won a Gold Glove, and had been named to three All-Star teams in his three years in Cleveland. Should he remain healthy, he would be the mainstay behind the plate for years to come. Against the wishes of his agent, Scott Boras, Sandy agreed to a five-year extension worth $11.35 million.

Hart then signed Paul Sorrento to a three-year, $2.1 million deal in January of 1993. Sorrento was a good buy at first base, earning the right to stay in the big leagues with a breakout year in '92. He hit 18 home runs over 140 games, and his on-base (.341), slugging (.443), and OPS (.784) percentages were all above the league average. This deal kept him under contract through the '95 season.

The next month, Cleveland extended Kenny Lofton to the tune of $6.3 million over four years, with a $4.25 million team option for 1997. The Lofton extension was a mega-deal, considering that the center fielder had just come over via trade from the Astros and had only played one full year in the big leagues. Even though he was still young, Lofton hit .285 for the Indians and set a record for AL rookies with 66 stolen bases. He had a promising career ahead of him, finishing second to Milwaukee shortstop Pat Listach in the Rookie of the Year voting.[1]

While the Indians were happy to pay up for Alomar, Sorrento, and Lofton, the most expensive deals belonged to Albert Belle and Carlos Baerga.

The left-fielder Belle got a four-year deal totaling $14.65 million. In three full seasons in the majors, Belle had been a menace to opposing pitching, averaging 33 homers and 112 runs batted in per year from 1991 to 1993.[2] He was named a Silver Slugger in '93, having launched 38 long-balls and driving in a major-league leading 129 RBI.

Even with those numbers, the largest deal went to second baseman Carlos Baerga. The front office had always expected Baerga to hit, which is why he was such an important acquisition in the Joe Carter trade of '89. But nobody could have predicted the type of output Baerga would bring to the number-three spot in the Indians order from '92 to '93. Baerga hit above .300 in back-to-back seasons (.312 and .321 respectively) with more than 200 hits and 20-plus home runs each year. It was a rare feat; one that had not been accomplished by a second baseman since Rogers Hornsby did it for the St. Louis Cardinals in 1922.[3] Baerga was halfway to matching Hornsby when the Indians inked him to a six-year deal at $21.4 million on April 7, 1993, which would keep him in Cleveland through the 1998 season, with a team option for 1999 at a price of about $4.7 million. The next day at Municipal Stadium, Baerga became the first man in baseball history to hit home runs from both

---

[1] In 1992, shortstop Pat Listach won the AL Rookie of the Year with a .290 batting average, 158 hits, an OBP of .352, and 54 stolen bases.

[2] Belle played in 62 games in 1989 and 9 in 1990, hitting a total of 8 home runs and 40 RBI.

[3] Since Baerga, other second basemen with seasons of .300/200 hits/20 HR/100 RBI include Bret Boone, Alfonso Soriano, Chase Utley and, most recently, Robinson Canó; however, it's a feat that none of them was able to duplicate.

sides of the plate in the same inning, doing so in the seventh against Yankees pitchers Steve Howe and Steve Farr.[4]

Sure, the Indians did end up missing the mark on some of the extensions they offered. But for every Charles Nagy, Carlos Baerga, and Sandy Alomar Jr. they extended, they also put together new deals for Mark Whiten, Jack Armstrong, Scott Scudder, Dave Otto, Glenalen Hill, Dennis Cook, Rod Nichols, Alex Cole, Carlos Martínez, Felix Fermín, and Thomas Howard. John Hart might have made some mistakes, but that was an understood risk, and one that Dick Jacobs was at peace with taking, given the opportunity cost. This was a groundbreaking movement. The Indians were the first team to sign its young players to long-term extensions, which has since become a common practice around baseball.

---

[4] Two other players have since homered twice in the same inning from different sides: Mark Bellhorn, for the Chicago Cubs, against the Milwaukee Brewers (August 29, 2002), and Kendrys Morales, for the Los Angeles Angels of Anaheim, against the Texas Rangers (July 30, 2012).

Chapter Seventeen

WINTER HAVEN AND THE BOAT ACCIDENT

"I hated leaving Tucson. I think everyone did."
—Mike Hargrove, former Indians manager

Spring training in Tucson was practically a rite of passage within the Indians' organization. The club had played exhibitions at Hi Corbett Field since the days of owner Bill Veeck in 1947. However, the decision to move to Florida was a no-brainer. Up through the start of the 1992 season, seventeen of the twenty-six major league teams held spring training in the Grapefruit League (Florida), while the Indians and six other squads were working out in the Cactus League (Arizona). There were the Brewers in Chandler; the Cubs were their neighbors to the north in Mesa; the A's ran camp due west in Phoenix; the Giants operated in the other end of the conurbation in Scottsdale; the Mariners were in Tempe (which was about to welcome the Angels); and the Padres were farthest away to the west in Yuma, less than 10 miles from the Mexican border.

Players and coaches enjoyed the desert climate, but missed out on a half or sometimes a full day's work because they had to leave their complexes at seven in the morning to bus along I-10 and across the desert for games. More teams and shorter trips in Florida allowed infielders to take more ground balls, extra time for pitchers to refine fundamentals in side sessions, additional batting practice, and the chance to get into a work routine that more closely mirrored that of the regular season.

But the Indians had never *planned* to move spring training to Winter Haven.

No, the ball club's original plans were to leave Arizona and the Cactus League behind to relocate farther south in the Sunshine State to Homestead, where the city had funded the construction of a $22 million facility in order to draw a major-league team to the area long-term for spring training. The Homestead Sports Complex featured a 6,500-seat stadium with a tropical salmon-colored wraparound façade and palm trees, five practice fields, training rooms, and dormitories to accommodate as many as 200 players. The Indians reached a deal with the city and had already begun moving some equipment and personnel to Florida when Hurricane Andrew made landfall in August of 1992. Homestead was directly in line with the Category 5 storm's path. With its winds whipping as quickly as 165 miles per hour, the hurricane leveled the state-of-the-art complex.

In all, Hurricane Andrew caused some $30 billion in property damage. The magnitude of the repairs required to resurrect the complex to working order were far too immense to have it ready in time for spring training in 1993. Team lawyers invoked an escape clause that was written into the contract with the city to look for a temporary place to play, but it left the organization with a conundrum: Where would the club move for the coming spring?

The Indians couldn't return to their familiar training grounds in Tucson, as the nascent Colorado Rockies had claimed the old complex to host their inaugural spring camp. And it's not like they could just *skip* spring training for a year (imagine which would have been worse, the media response to a decision like that or the on-field results stemming from it).

There was, however, another option tucked away in the middle of the Grapefruit League in central Florida that would continue to allow the club to train in the state. The Red Sox were moving to a new complex in Ft. Myers, and would be leaving Chain of Lakes Park vacant in Winter Haven, where they had conducted spring training dating back to 1966. It was a much older complex (it happened to be the ballpark where John Hart played in his first professional game as a minor leaguer in the Expos system), but would suffice for the time-being.

The only catch was that the city wanted to be sure that it could retain whichever team became its tenant, so what the Indians' hoped would only be a short-term fix would have to be at least a ten-year commitment. So essentially, they'd never have a chance to use the complex built for them in Homestead. But seeing no other alternative, they agreed to the deal. Wanting to be hospitable, the mayor of Winter Haven, the Honorable Ellie Threlkel, and her husband, Dr. Jim, welcomed Dick Jacobs, John Hart, Tom Giordano, and Dennis Lehman to town with open arms, hosting them to a reception upon their arrival. The city did some updating and repainting around the stadium and was ready for the Tribe when the club reported for camp in February.

"People don't know what a marvelous gem this little ballpark is," Hart said, addressing the crowd at the Indians' spring opener. The organization didn't realize how productive their players and coaches could be at the facility either until after the move. There was an extra practice field and two batting cages—including a new cage structure along the right-field line—and unlike Tucson, Winter Haven placed the Indians in close proximity to other teams. The Braves, Reds and Tigers, for example, were all within forty-five minutes of the complex.

"It was easier to get it all done in Winter Haven, much more conducive," Hargrove says about the move. "The players responded well to it. We got in some good, intense work. After the day was over, you could keep two or three guys for extra batting practice or by the clubhouse before games."

A typical day in Winter Haven began with stretching and aerobics at 9 a.m. Then the team broke into groups on the six fields, rotating stations every twenty-five minutes. Four groups of position players had two minutes to run and ready themselves at the next field whenever the air horn sounded. It trumpeted a second time to signal the coaches and instructors that they were on the clock and to carry on with their prescribed exercises at each station. Coaches hit sharp liners and choppy grounders to fielders at some defensive stations, or had players track and snare fly balls at others; coaches threw batting practice on fields or in the cages; pitchers threw live batting practice sessions to simulate real at-bats on some of the adjacent fields and rotated in and out of the six-pack of mounds; and all players ran and used the weight room. The training was arduous, but the players made noticeable strides with the regimen.

Dick Jacobs took note of this. The move to Florida allowed the owner an opportunity to start a tradition of his own: flying forty to fifty business leaders from Cleveland to Winter Haven on his company plane. It would be the same group every year, with the heads of the city's top legal firms, hospitals, and businesses making the trip. Dick never went unnoticed on those trips, especially when he lingered around the batting cage, sporting his signature yellow dress pants and white shoes. He took plenty of ribbing for it from his center fielder, Kenny Lofton, who was critical of the owner's fashion tastes. Mr. Jacobs laughed off the comments and flew his entourage to his Pier House Resort in Key West, where they finished their annual spring getaway.

Now given the quantity and the quality of work being put in that spring, the players and coaches were looking forward to getting a day off to rest and enjoy their families away from the ballpark . . . but the front office wasn't as eager to grant their reprieve.

"Hart and O'Dowd were real task masters," recalls Dr. Bill Wilder, the Indians team physician at the time. "They wanted the team to work out and have no off-days during spring training."

But they relented on March 22, 1993.

* * *

The phone rang at manager Mike Hargrove's apartment in Winter Haven at about 9 p.m. He and his wife, Sharon, had pitching coach Rick Adair, his wife Lou, their boys, and some friends over for company. The manager got up and excused himself to take the call. On the other end of the line was Fernando Montes, the strength and conditioning coach of the Indians. His message was harrowing. There had been an accident involving three pitchers who had taken a boat out on a lake in the town of Clermont, and the scene was grisly. After hearing the news, Hargrove and Adair's families climbed into their cars and drove to the lake to see what had taken place.

Little Lake Nellie is your typical Florida lake, just like any other of the 500-plus rounded or oblong bodies of water that dot the center of the state. It's quiet. Cypress and orange trees circle the perimeter. Reeds poke up from the surface along the edges. There's a tranquil quality about such a pastoral place. That's part of the reason why pitcher Tim Crews and his wife, Laurie, chose to buy their home there. Tim left the Los Angeles Dodgers, with whom he had spent all six of his major-league seasons, and signed with Cleveland exactly two months earlier in January. He and his wife, both Florida natives, found a cedar house that sat on 45 acres of rolling green grass situated on the lake in Clermont, less than an hour north of the Indians' complex. It was their dream house, complete with stables, corrals, fences, and horses for them to enjoy with their three children.

The Crews picnicked at their home on the lake that afternoon. Tim invited Montes, two teammates, and their families over to join. One was Bobby Ojeda, a thirty-five-year-old pitcher, whom the Indians had signed three months prior to slate into the No. 2 spot in the starting rotation. Ojeda was a member of the 1986 world champion Mets, and had been Crews' teammate for the last two seasons in Los Angeles. The other was Steve Olin, a twenty-seven-year-old right-hander with a sidearm delivery who had made his way up through the Indians' organization before eventually becoming the closer for the club in 1991. Olin led the team in saves during his two campaigns as the stopper.[1]

The families barbecued and took turns riding horses. Around dusk, the trio of pitchers piled into Crews' boat for some night fishing while their wives stayed behind to watch after the children. Laurie cautioned Tim about it being too dark to take the boat out on the water, but he insisted. It was supposed to be nothing more than a relaxing way to end their day off.

Montes had been on the boat but had the apparent misfortune of losing a game of "Rock, Paper, Scissors," which they played to decide which man had to disembark from the vessel to go retrieve the fishing gear. (That was the last time he ever played that game.) One of Tim's friends was supposed to be joining them later as well. He flashed the lights on his truck from the shoreline when he arrived so they would come back in and pick him up. That's when Tim sped around the lake a few times in his Skeeter, an 18-foot open bass fishing boot, before revving it toward the shore. But as dusk turned to darkness on what was already an overcast night, he never saw the wooden dock extending almost 200 feet into the water. The boat tore through the dock, hitting almost at head-level, knocking off the pilings, and coming to rest almost 100 feet past the structure. The cacophony brought neighbors into their yards. One summoned paramedics.

The children were still running around and playing inside the home when Hargrove, Adair, and their families pulled up the dirt driveway.

"It was surreal," Hargrove remembers. "They had no idea that their world had just been up-ended."

Sharon Hargrove embraced Patti Olin, Steve's wife. Patti, twenty-six, was the mother of a three-year-old and a set of six-month-old twins. Her husband's head had slammed into the pier when the boat crashed, killing him instantly. Crews and Ojeda were airlifted to separate hospitals.

John Hart and Danny O'Dowd arrived an hour or two later, and Sharon and Lou took Patti and the kids back to the Hargroves' place in Winter Haven.

---

[1] Olin recorded 17 saves in the '91 season and 29 in '92.

Hart, O'Dowd, and the coaches went to Orlando Regional Medical Center to check on Crews, while Ojeda had been taken to South Lake Memorial Hospital in Clermont. Ojeda's injuries were the least serious, and he would have been decapitated had he not been slouched over in the boat. It saved his life, but as a result, the top of his head had been scalped back like an orange peel. Two quarts of his blood spilled onto the deck as he knelt over Crews' body, urging him to keep fighting and stay alive. But when Crews' mother and father met Indians personnel in the hospital waiting room, they told them that their Timmy's chances were not looking good. Crews didn't make it to daybreak, dying from injuries sustained to his head and lungs. A toxicology report later revealed that his blood alcohol level had been .14, which was well above Florida's legal limit.

The last thing the Indians organization expected to have after a rare off-day was two of their players dead and a third clinging to life. It gave Hargrove too much to think about in the early morning. He couldn't bring himself to sleep, though he hadn't gotten any shuteye in over twenty-four hours. He had been so shocked and distraught that he'd almost driven his car off the road when his family first headed to the lake house to assess the situation. The manager felt partially responsible, as he was the one who lobbied for the off-day. Hargrove had rejected the notion of playing an unscheduled exhibition game with the Dodgers, something that John Hart and longtime Los Angeles skipper Tommy Lasorda tried arranging; he knew how much it meant for his players to have their only day free from baseball activities. Now he was vowing to never schedule another spring-training off-day for the rest of his tenure as manager. He wasn't sure how he was going to look at his team and rally the roster to get through such a tragedy. Therefore, instead of returning home from the hospital, Hargrove headed straight to the ballpark before sunup. And just as he extended his hand toward the doorknob to open the clubhouse, it dawned on him that he still had no clue what he was going to say to his players when they arrived.

* * *

There's ordinarily a sense of machismo that runs rampant around most clubhouses. Baseball tradition lionizes the players who outmuscle opponents in the batter's box, spit saliva darkened by the wads of tobacco packed tightly in their lips, and bristle at emotional displays that convey even the slightest tinge of weakness. Grown men crying and hugging? That's not the culture of baseball. Just think of Jimmy Dugan (Tom Hanks) in *A League of Their Own*, yelling "There's no crying in baseball!" But that mentality no longer existed in the Indians' locker room as soon as it was faced with this catastrophe.

Hargrove stopped at the doorstep and said a prayer before entering.

Lord, he thought to himself, *Help me through this so I say something that makes sense.* It occurred to him shortly thereafter that he didn't necessarily have to say much at all.

"Get four baseball players together and they can tell stories 'til the cows come home," he explains, recalling that morning. And that's precisely what they did. The players circled their chairs around the clubhouse and began reliving memories and grieving as one baseball family. A player would talk for as long as he wished or was able to, and another teammate would pick up wherever he left off. Even when there was nothing left to be said, there were reminders of their loss everywhere Hargrove looked, particularly of Olin. The other relievers memorialized him; he was one of their own. Heck, they even referred to themselves together as "The Bullpen." Eric Plunk wore one of Olin's T-shirts. Ted Power wore his belt, the same one he'd worn when he had his major-league call-up in July of 1989. Derek Lilliquist held two steel balls, which Olin had used to strengthen his wrists. Kevin Wickander wore the right-hander's shower shoes. Olin had even been the best man at Wickander's wedding. Tim Crews had only just recently joined the team and they didn't know him any better than for a guy with a smiling face and a curvy mustache who would've made a good teammate.

Then there was Ojeda. Hargrove couldn't deny the player's request to talk to the team. It was a courageous act, but it made the tragedy even more real. Here was living proof that they could all reach out and touch. Here was Bobby Ojeda's ghastly apparition. His complexion was pallid and all traces of vibrancy were gone from his eyes. His head was bandaged and wrapped, concealing the cuts that left his forehead grooved like baseball seams. The air got sucked out of the room when he mustered the strength to appear in the clubhouse.

The Indians organization held a memorial service in Winter Haven to begin the formal grieving process two days later. Every team in baseball sent a representative to the ceremony. Steve Olin had once told his wife that the Garth Brooks song "The Dance" should be the song played at his funeral.

Looking back on the memory of
The dance we shared beneath the stars above
For a moment all the world was right.
How could I have known that you'd ever say goodbye?
And now I'm glad I didn't know
The way it all would end, the way it all would go.
Our lives are better left to chance, I could have missed the pain
But I'd of had to miss the dance.

The lyrics moved the crowd to tears when it was played over the loud-speakers at Chain of Lakes Park.

As a sign of goodwill, Mayor Threlkel and the City of Winter Haven presented two palm trees to be planted and a plaque dedicated to the departed players. The trees and the memorial marker even followed the Indians when they moved spring training to Goodyear, Arizona, sixteen years later in 2009.

The ball club looked for a sense of purpose as it worked through the rest of spring training, but struggled mildly. The Hargrove's even went so far as to open their doors to players, personnel, and families at their apartment for the rest of camp. Suddenly, everyone's shoulder became one to cry on.

When the Indians returned to Cleveland, the team honored the Olin and Crews families at home plate before the opener at Municipal Stadium.

Players sported patches on their uniform sleeves with a baseball containing the pitchers' numbers. Olin's No. 31 had an upward-pointing arrow placed above it, while a star accompanied Crews' No. 52. And to start the season, on April 5, 1993, the Yankees shellacked the Tribe, 9–1, in front of 73,290 heartbroken fans.

Ojeda did eventually make a return to action, but not before fleeing to Sweden unannounced, hoping to escape his depression and the devastating reminders of his life before the accident. He came back to Cleveland to have plastic surgery performed to correct his scar, go through rehabilitation and, with the support of Patti Olin, Laurie Crews, family, friends, and teammates, wore his Indians uniform again by the end of June.

However, the losing continued for as long as the Indians grieved during the first half of the season. Cleveland lost 43 of its first 81 games. The players looked listless in the field and made errors in bunches (71 such gaffes to be exact). But the manager couldn't find it in himself to be too hard on them. Just when he thought he could, Hargrove remembered their tears. The accident had given them an opportunity to see sides of each other that they had never seen with any other organization. This fostered lifelong bonds that further instilled the Indians' sense of family in the second half, much less the rest of the decade.

Chapter Eighteen

THE CONTINUING SAGA OF ALBERT BELLE, PART II

Let's try to find ten *good* things to say about Albert Belle:

10. So far as we know, he's never killed anyone.
9. He is handsome, and built like a god.
8. He played every game.
7. He has never appeared on the *Jerry Springer Show*.
6. He was an underrated base runner who was rarely caught stealing.
5. He hasn't been arrested in several years.
4. He is very bright.
3. He works hard.
2. He has never spoken favorably about Adolf Hitler, Saddam Hussein, or any other foreign madman.
1. The man could hit.

> —Noted sabermetrician Bill James' entry for Albert Belle in the top-100 left fielders, from *The New Bill James Historical Abstract*

Even as the new-and-improved Albert Belle continued to destroy opposing pitching, he remained prone to lashing out. It was known that he liked the clubhouse thermostat to chill below 60 degrees. Teammates started calling him "Mr. Freeze" because he smashed a thermostat after somebody turned up the heat. Other times, he victimized postgame meal spreads, sending dishes flying into the showers. On one occasion, still unsatisfied after a frustrating plate appearance against the Red Sox, he took a bat to Kenny Lofton's boom box in the visitor's clubhouse at Fenway Park.

There came a point when Dick Jacobs brought the slugger's behavior to question during a budget meeting with Mike Hargrove, John Hart, Dan O'Dowd, and some assistants. The owner looked at the manager and asked, "Can this ball club win without Albert Belle?"

Hargrove thought that it was a pretty good question. If you put aside the off-the-field issues, Albert could flat-out hit.

"Mr. Jacobs," he answered, "yes, we can win without him . . . but he makes it a whole lot easier."

Hargrove knew that legitimate, contending teams always had that one hitter in the middle of their lineup who was a monster; and for the Indians, Albert Belle was that monster. He outwardly exuded it, too, projecting it at the other teams' pitchers. He was always flexing—and did he ever have the muscles to be able to do that. Belle was a physical specimen; a guy built like a middle linebacker who started in left field.

"At the plate, he had that look of, 'I'm getting ready to tear your throat out and s**t it down your windpipe,'" Hargrove said. Pitchers around the league learned to fear that look.

And Belle gave them good reason to be fearful. During his time in an Indians uniform, he charged mounds, confronted fans, yelled at media (the Hannah Storm incident) and blew off an invitation from Ted Williams to attend an event honoring baseball's top hitters.[1] He even got in his car and

---

[1] Albert Belle launched into a profanity-laced rant directed at reporters, especially television broadcaster Hannah Storm of NBC, who tried conducting pregame interviews with

chased down teenagers who egged his house on Halloween after the '95 World Series. Most people—the media, the fans, opposing teams—saw Belle for his explosive tantrums, as well as gargantuan home runs. However, what they didn't see was how hard he worked. His competitive drive made him a polarizing figure in certain situations and occasional frustrations caused him to gnash his teeth, making him a danger to people and property around him. The Indians billed him $10,000 a season for damages in clubhouses at home and on the road, only putting up with his misbehavior because of his stellar numbers.

Hitting coaches often speak of instant amnesia or flushing previous at-bats from short-term memory. They are mental terms that are ordinarily thrown around to help hitters cope with failures at the plate and regain focus. Belle, on the other hand, was extreme, and applied that mental concept to his preparation, even if the previous at-bat resulted in a favorable outcome. Rick Wolff found him in the batting cages under Yankee Stadium after crushing a no-doubt-about-it homer. A Ruthian blast in the house that he had built.

Albert set a ball on a tee and hit it into the net.

"What are you doing down here hitting?" Wolff asked with a sound of wonderment evident in his voice. "You just hit a homer."

Belle replaced the ball on the tee with another one before he started to explain. Sure, he hit a home run, but he didn't hit the ball *right*. It might have carried far enough for everyone else to call it a tape-measure blast, but he wasn't thrilled with his contact. And because he was penciled in the lineup as the designated hitter that day, he had time to fix it before he went up to bat again.

---

his teammates prior to Game 3 of the 1995 World Series. Commissioner Bud Selig fined Belle $50,000 for the incident. Belle supposedly issued an apology through a statement released by the Indians, saying, "I very much regret the incident and the ill feelings it has generated. At no time whatsoever was the presence in the dugout of any individual reporter the cause of my actions. I was upset with the sheer number of them in the dugout and not any particular one. But, having said that, many of them were simply doing their job, and it was not for me to decide that they should not be there." Then he turned around and told *Newsweek* that he took no responsibility for the statement, saying, "I told them to take it out. I apologize for nothing."

Wolff shrugged his shoulders and walked away. Albert took his cuts down below in the batting cage for another fifteen minutes before reemerging in the dugout. Relating the story, Wolff helped Hargrove understand what really drove Belle, what sparked his inner drive, and how to tap into that. "The good clubs police themselves," Hargrove says.

Everybody on the team had a hook, and it was Hargrove's job as the manager to find it. He needed to get to Belle, and the hook he found was simple arithmetic. Belle had always worked well with numbers; he did, after all, study accounting at LSU. And apparently he knew every all-time offensive stat in Indians franchise history, committing them to memory. He knew that Earl Averill hit the most home runs (226) and runs batted in (1,084). Or that Tris Speaker's 486 doubles were more than any other man to wear the Cleveland uniform. He could rattle off "Shoeless" Joe Jackson's name as the owner of the highest team batting average, at a .375 clip.

Albert wanted to be all of those things; a leader in every category. He also wanted to be talked to like a man. So Hargrove called him into his office and sat him down.

"You have Hall-of-Fame talent, Albert," he told his slugger. "You *should* put up huge offensive numbers. But to do that, you need to be in the lineup and get your at-bats."

That was Hargrove's entire point. As good as his bat was, he could really be a pain. Albert knew from his previous benchings and demotions that the manager would be true to his word.

Hargrove made it clear that if Albert didn't shape up, he wouldn't be able to pursue those statistical benchmarks and achieve the superior place in the record books as he wanted.

"You will leave me with no choice but to take you out of the lineup, and you don't get to accomplish your goals," he said. "So do us both a favor and don't do those things."

That was the ultimatum he offered, and that's when the message finally hit home. And though he was never fully cured of it, Albert Belle became less colicky and began limiting his tantrums.

Chapter Nineteen

THE OMAR VIZQUEL TRADE

A truism in baseball is that competitive teams are designed to have strong defenses up through the middle of the field, and John Hart could do no better than by acquiring Omar Vizquel.

The Indians' starting shortstop in 1993 was Felix Fermín, a thirty-year-old from the Dominican Republic who had just finished signing a contract extension earlier in the year. Fermín was coming off an especially productive season in which he established career highs in hits (126), doubles (16), home runs (2) and RBI (45). His superior strikeout ratio (one K in every 36.7 at-bats) was the best in the majors that season; but in the field, the Indians could stand for an upgrade. Fermín had below-average range at shortstop and ranked in the top five for errors committed at the position.[1]

The Indians had attempted to trade Fermín and a pitcher, twenty-two-year-old right-hander Albie Lopez, to the New York Mets over the Winter Meetings. The Mets wanted a veteran shortstop and were willing to give up right-handed starter Bret Saberhagen to complete the deal. The thought

---

[1] Fermín led the team with 23 errors.

of adding Saberhagen was enticing: He was a two-time Cy Young Award winner (1985, 1989), and had been named World Series MVP after helping Kansas City win it all in 1985. An obstacle that might have prevented the deal was a deferred payment clause in Saberhagen's contract, which called for him to receive $250,000 per year for twenty years in addition to the $15.34 million from the extension he signed with the Mets the previous spring. As the Indians were also interested in Astros pitchers Doug Drabek and Pete Harnisch, the organization ultimately walked away from the Saberhagen deal.

John conceived another trade involving Fermín and another infielder, Reggie Jefferson, after the Winter Meetings. He had already started talking to Seattle's general manager, Woody Woodward, about a potential deal that would bring the Mariners' young shortstop, Omar Vizquel, to Cleveland. It's a discussion the pair of executives had while they attended a function second baseman Carlos Baerga was hosting in his native Puerto Rico. However, Hart didn't make a real push for the trade until *after* he had run into the M's designated hitter, Edgar Martínez, at Baerga's event.

The two started chatting about their clubs, but Hart was careful not to get to the heart of his trade talks. He prodded, saying, "Edgar, tell me a little bit about Jay Buhner," and the DH said some things about the right fielder. "What about Randy Johnson?" Hart said, baiting him along, before making a conciliatory assertion. "Boy, I really like your club. You've got Alex Rodriguez coming up." That finally had brought him to the shortstop position, where the conversation drifted to Omar, and Edgar Martínez couldn't say a bad thing about him.

"You know, John, this guy is special," he said. "He's really a glue for our club. I know we've got this young shortstop coming, but boy, Vizquel is special."

Omar Vizquel was indeed special. He had just won his first Gold Glove award and was a sharp fielder who made even the toughest plays look routine.[2] He could dart to his left and right, barehanding line drives and

---

[2] Vizquel would go on to win ten more Gold Glove awards (1993–2001, 2005–2006) during his twenty-four-year career.

making throws on the run. That sort of play was typical of Omar, who refined his trade as a youngster using a makeshift glove he fashioned from milk cartons to practice snatching ground balls in a rocky field littered with broken glass and trash in his native Caracas, Venezuela. Those skills would pair nicely for a double-play combination with Baerga, as Carlos could turn two by using his arm strength alone.

Based on that, John Hart didn't need to hear any more. He was sold on Vizquel and finalized a deal that night with Woody Woodward, sending Felix Fermín, Reggie Jefferson, and cash considerations to Seattle. Edgar wasn't too thrilled the next day when he learned the news. He walked over to John and started to tell him, "You're no good!" Martínez was really upset about it, but soon resigned himself and conceded, "You really got a great player."

Mike Hargrove agreed. With Sandy Alomar Jr. behind the plate, Omar Vizquel at shortstop, and Kenny Lofton in center field, his team had a Gold Glove winner at each position through the middle of the field. And with the bats he had coming through the lineup and this defensive arrangement, he thought he might soon see his team emerge as a contender. To the Indians' credit, so did their opponents.

Future Hall of Famer Sparky Anderson made a comment to Hargrove to validate this belief. The Tigers' skipper pulled him aside at the ballpark and said, "Mike, you guys are real close to being really good." It meant the world to Hargrove to hear that from another manager, much less one of Sparky's stature. Anderson knew a talented team when he saw one: His 2,194 career victories rank sixth all-time among major-league managers, and he was the first ever to manage a team to victory in the World Series in both leagues, having led Cincinnati's "Big Red Machine" in the seventies and the Detroit Tigers in the eighties.[3]

---

[3] Tony LaRussa became only the second manager in MLB history to have won the World Series with teams from both leagues. LaRussa piloted the Oakland A's to victory in the 1989 Series, and won twice with the St. Louis Cardinals (in 2006 and 2011).

Members of the front office also began drawing positive remarks from other teams' personnel. Yankees manager Buck Showalter called Hart once with words of encouragement after his squad swept the Indians.

"Boy, I'll tell you, I see trouble brewing in Cleveland," Buck said. "That's as talented a group of young players as I've ever seen."

Bob Engle, the scouting director for the Blue Jays, confessed to Mickey White that he was beginning to feel threatened whenever he would show up at a ballpark and found Cleveland's scouts already there. Engle said he had never felt that way before, either.

Hart, O'Dowd, White, and Hargrove all appreciated the flattery, as they were also beginning to see the fruits of their labor. However, they also agreed that they were still missing a few established players to put their team over the edge as a legitimate title contender. This meant it was time for them to launch into another phase of the five-year plan. It was time to go shopping.

The Indians' motorcade cruises along the parade route into downtown Cleveland in October of 1948, the last time the franchise won the World Series. *Photo courtesy of the Cleveland Indians*

Former Indians owner Bill Veeck "weeps" as Indians players and members of the front office bury the '48 championship pennant at Cleveland Municipal Stadium. Veeck staged the event as a promotion after the team had been mathematically eliminated from repeating as champions in September of 1949. *Photo courtesy of the Cleveland Indians*

Bob Feller won 266 games for the Indians from 1936–56, including six season with 20 or more victories. He was inducted in the National Baseball Hall of Fame in 1962. *Photo courtesy of the Cleveland Indians*

Rocky Colavito won over the Indians' fan base en route to claiming the 1959 home-run title in the American League. Former general manager Frank Lane promptly traded him to the Detroit Tigers in March of 1960 for the '59 batting champion, Harvey Kuenn. Thereafter, the Indians didn't finish better than 11 games out of first place until 1994, giving rise to the alleged "Curse of Rocky Colavito." *Photo courtesy of the Cleveland Indians*

Henry J. "Hank" Peters was introduced as president and general manager of the Indians after the 1987 season. He retired from baseball in September of 1991 after a career spanning four decades, and was succeeded by his protégé, John Hart. *Photo courtesy of the Cleveland Indians*

Situated on the Lake Erie shoreline, the cavernous Municipal Stadium served as the home of the Indians from 1932–93, and the Browns' NFL franchise from 1946–95. Often referred to as "The Mistake on the Lake," it was demolished in 1996. *Photo courtesy of the Cleveland Indians*

Brawny slugger Albert Belle, shown here at Municipal Stadium, often upstaged pitchers with his menacing scowl from the batter's box. *Photo courtesy of the Cleveland Indians*

Carlos Baerga recorded back-to-back seasons hitting above .300 with 200 hits, 20 homers, and 100 RBI from 1992–93, becoming the first second baseman since Rogers Hornsby in 1922 to accomplish the feat. *Photo courtesy of the Cleveland Indians*

Jim Thome's pre-pitch routine included pointing his bat toward the field like Roy Hobbs (Robert Redford) in *The Natural*; a strategy hitting coach Charlie Manuel offered after his rookie season. The Indians' all-time leader in home runs, Thome clubbed 337 of his 612 career blasts wearing a Tribe uniform.
Photo courtesy of the Cleveland Indians

Manny Ramírez showcased his sweet swing with the Indians from 1993–2000. Ramírez went on to tally 555 home runs in his career. He won two World Series as a member of the Boston Red Sox. *Photo courtesy of the Cleveland Indians*

Former owner Richard E. "Dick" Jacobs promised Cleveland a new baseball park for the Indians, and he delivered with the state-of-the-art Jacobs Field, which opened in 1994. *Photo courtesy of The Plain Dealer/Landov*

A sellout crowd packed Jacobs Field for its first regular-season game on April 4, 1994. The Indians beat the Seattle Mariners, 4–3, in 11 innings. *Photo courtesy of AP Images*

President Bill Clinton took the mound to throw out the ceremonial first pitch and inaugurate the new stadium on Opening Day of 1994. *Photo courtesy of AP Images*

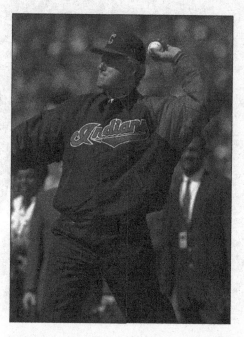

Outfielder Kenny Lofton was a fixture atop the Indians lineup and in center field, where he won four Gold Glove awards. Lofton also led the AL in stolen bases each year from 1992–96. *Photo courtesy of the Cleveland Indians*

Omar Vizquel leaps to snare a line drive at shortstop. Vizquel dazzled with his defensive play, winning nine of eleven Gold Gloves as a member of the Indians. *Photo courtesy of the Cleveland Indians*

Former manager Mike Hargrove (right, beside Kenny Lofton) won 721 games with the Indians, seven short of Lou Boudreau's franchise-best 728 victories. *Photo courtesy of the Cleveland Indians*

Designated hitter Eddie Murray connects for his 3,000th hit on June 30, 1995, against Minnesota Twins pitcher Mike Trombley at the Hubert H. Humphrey Metrodome. *Photo courtesy of the Cleveland Indians*

One night after clinching their first playoff berth in forty-one years,
the Indians claimed the AL Central crown on September 8, 1995.
Photo courtesy of the Cleveland Indians

Albert Belle meets with reporters as the Indians celebrate their first
division title since 1954. *Photo courtesy of the Cleveland Indians*

Kenny Lofton jumps to celebrate scoring a run during the Indians' streak to the AL pennant in October of 1995. *Photo courtesy of the Cleveland Indians*

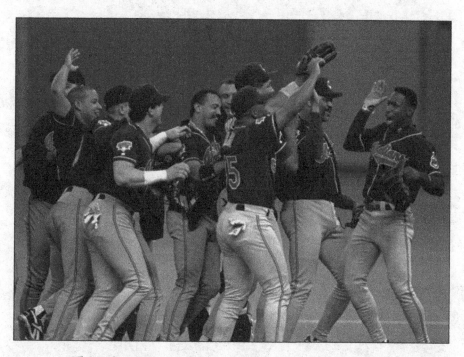

The Indians pour onto the field at the Seattle Kingdome to celebrate after winning the AL championship over the Mariners in six games. *Photo courtesy of AP Images*

Jim Thome and Orel Hershiser wave to the fans during an Interview with ABC's John Saunders before Game 3 of the 1995 World Series in Cleveland. *Photo courtesy of the Cleveland Indians*

Fans cheer for the Tribe during a rally at Public Square in Cleveland on the eve of the 1995 World Series. The Atlanta Braves went on to defeat the Indians, four games to two. *Photo courtesy of AP Images*

Second baseman Carlos Baerga pumps his fists after starting a rally with an eleventh-inning double, which helped the Indians to victory in Game 3 of the 1995 World Series. *Photo courtesy of the Cleveland Indians*

(left to right) Kenny Lofton, Albert Belle, and Carlos Baerga pose for a photo during spring training at Chain of Lakes Park in Winter Haven, Florida. *Photo courtesy of AP Images*

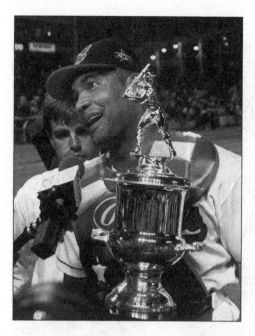

Catcher Sandy Alomar Jr. accepts his trophy after being named the Most Valuable Player at the 1997 All-Star Game in Cleveland. Alomar's two-run homer gave the American League the lead in their 3–1 victory. *Photo courtesy of AP Images*

Closer José Mesa, catcher Sandy Alomar Jr., and first baseman Jim Thome celebrate the Indians' victory on October 10, 1997, over the New York Yankees in the American League Division Series. Cleveland advanced to the American League Championship and World Series for the second time in three years. *Photo courtesy of AP Images*

Former general manager John Hart speaking at his induction into the Indians' Distinguished Hall of Fame on June 22, 2013, in Cleveland. *Photo courtesy of the Cleveland Indians*

Chapter Twenty

BUYER'S MARKET

Exploring the buyer's market was relatively uncharted territory for the Indians with John Hart at the helm. Cleveland was never used to being the club making big splashes and drawing up contracts for proven, sought-after talent. One supposes the front office *could* have gone after the sampling of free agents a year or two earlier, like in 1992, when the market was chock-full of A-listers at every position. Almost a half-dozen players who would later be enshrined in the Hall of Fame in Cooperstown were free agents before or after the '92 campaign. Outfielders Andre Dawson and Dave Winfield changed teams (Dawson left the Cubs and signed with the Red Sox, while Winfield departed the Blue Jays to join the Twins). Reliever Rich "Goose" Gossage resigned in Oakland, and shortstops Robin Yount and Ozzie Smith stayed put with their respective teams, the Brewers and Cardinals.[1] A sixth eventual Hall of Famer, Montreal Expos catcher Gary Carter, fought back tears at the end of the season as he announced his intention to retire.

---

[1] After fifteen major-league seasons, the 1992 off-season marked the first time in Smith's career that he was a free agent. He re-signed with the Cardinals a month later.

There were other notables on the market, including outfielders Chili Davis and Kevin Bass, as well as the Tigers' double-play tandem of Alan Trammell and Lou Whitaker. However, no matter how much the Indians might have wanted to pursue those free agents, John Hart made no such move; sitting patiently and passing on those options. The most he did was negotiate a handful of minor-league deals, as it was still somewhat early in the framework of his plans to delve into the free-agent market.

That said, one item was becoming very clear to the general manager: Pitching was the area in which his team would need the most immediate improvement. The Indians organization saw the signs that it would soon have a masher of a club in the big leagues, but their pitching was an entirely different story. Charles Nagy would have been adequate as a good No. 3 starter in most other American League rotations, but he was pegged as the Indians' ace moving forward. The former first-round pick was coming off his first All-Star campaign, in which he won 17 games and posted a 2.96 ERA. Cleveland's staff logged 1,470 innings pitched in '92 (the most in the league), but finished in the bottom half in nearly every other statistical category. On some days, it looked like the Tribe's pitchers were throwing batting practice to opposing lineups. The staff gave up a league-worst 159 home runs and was tagged for more than 1,500 hits, the second-highest total in the Junior Circuit. Hart had signed a few players to address some of the pitching concerns after the season, but the only signing that really panned out in the long run was Eric Plunk, who evolved into a dependable set-up man with a mid-90s fastball. Plunk, who had been a part of Oakland's pennant run in '88, signed his deal with the Indians in November, very early into the offseason. The next month was when Cleveland had signed Bobby Ojeda, and after the horror at Little Lake Nellie, left town after one season.

The front office got much more aggressive following the 1993 season after the staff consulted players and coaches. They, too, saw the need for a handful of veteran players; guys who had been there and could finally put the Indians in the hunt. They specifically requested that Hart sign three or four key guys with an ability to lead on and off the field. The pitching was still going to be a focal point in the dealing, as it needed to be. Nagy, still regarded as the ace, threw fewer than fifty innings in 1993 and scuttled to a 2–6 record after missing most of the year with arm problems. José Mesa's 10 wins were the most on staff, but those wins went with a dozen losses. In fact, Mark Clark was the only regular starter with a winning record (7–5). The club's pitching numbers had declined as a whole, something that shouldn't have been possible given the poor performance during the previous season. With that in mind, Hart added two proven arms to the starting rotation.

The first was Dennis Martínez, who had recently completed a 15–9 season in Montreal. He represented the Expos with a trio of All-Star appearances, hurled a perfect game against the Dodgers, and was a part of Hank Peters' championship squad in Baltimore that won the '83 World Series. Nicknamed "El Presidente," Martínez also had the distinction of being one of only seven pitchers in MLB history to win one hundred games in each league. The signing of Martínez required some courtship from the front office and Indians ownership, as he never used to like coming to Cleveland during his time with the Orioles. "The place was dead long before Jacobs took over," he recalls.

Cleveland didn't have the type of allure and excitement that most professional athletes flock to. The nightlife after a ball game wasn't much to write home about, especially prior to the development of the Flats district. The perpetual gray skies and the biting wind chill off of Lake Erie were a far cry from the tropical setting of Martínez' native Nicaragua.

The Indians assured him that was all about to change. John Hart took him for a tour of the club's new ballpark four months before it was set to open. The Tribe's high-powered offense would be another critical selling point to woo Martínez. He would benefit from a bevy of run support from a lineup loaded with sluggers, and that was music to any pitcher's ears.

The owner's generosity also sent a very unexpected message to the pitcher that he belonged in Cleveland. After Martínez agreed to terms in December, the Indians planned to unveil their newest horse at a press conference at their soon-to-be-finished stadium. Martínez was expecting to be in

Miami for a family reunion, and he told the management that he would not be able to attend their announcement. But Dick Jacobs approached Martínez and told him how much it meant for him to be there. He had waited a long time for his club to announce a signing like that of Martínez.

"Don't worry about it," the owner said. "My plane will take you back to Miami. I'd like to have you there for the announcement."

Dennis was taken aback by the gesture and was extraordinarily grateful for his new boss' openhandedness.

"It was the first time in my career that I thought, *Well, I am dealing with the right people here*," Martínez says.

The right-hander signed a two-year contract worth a guaranteed $9 million, which included a $4.25 million option for a third season. Starting pitching was in demand, and the Yankees and Rangers had also pursued Martínez, which drove up his market price. But after the Indians lost out on bids for two other free-agent pitchers (Sid Fernandez, who signed with the Orioles, and Mark Portugal, who ended up going to San Francisco), Hart was content to have gotten an established front-line pitcher and a tested leader for what he deemed to be affordable dollars.

The second pitcher the Indians signed heading into the '94 season arrived in February, two weeks before the club opened camp in Winter Haven. By then, Jack Morris was well past his prime. His performance in '93 was one of the worst showings of his career, and it was an item of stark contrast when compared against his league-best 21 wins in '92. Morris had struggled to stay healthy, and there had even been so much doubt surrounding him that the Blue Jays bought out the final year of his contract for a million dollars. But Morris still wanted to prove that he could go to the mound and compete. He had a track record to prove his worth as a big-game pitcher; after all, Morris had won five postseason starts for the Twins in '91, and his ten shutout innings against the Atlanta Braves in the pivotal game of the World Series were still relatively fresh in people's minds. Especially after he was named World Series MVP for his mastery.

The Indians shared some of the same concerns as Morris' former employer, but still needed to add an arm to their arsenal. In discussions, Hart praised Morris for his makeup and intangibles, and hoped he would work out for the better in Cleveland. The club decided it would make the pitcher earn his right to a swan song in an Indians uniform, offering Morris $350,000 if he were to make the Opening Day roster. The front office drew up a contract that was heavy on incentives to hedge its bets. The thirty-nine-year-old could make as much as $2.6 million if he made a return to form, in which case the Indians would not have any buyer's remorse.[2]

Cleveland also made two significant acquisitions of position players prior to opening the '94 campaign. One was first baseman Eddie Murray, who, like his former Orioles teammate Dennis Martínez, signed on with the Indians in December. Until then, "Steady Eddie" had spent twelve of his seventeen years of major-league service in Baltimore, where he earned a reputation as a reliable and productive switch hitter. The Indians expected Eddie would continue as an offensive weapon even at age thirty-eight, bookending Albert Belle in the middle of the lineup. While they hoped his bat still had some pop, the Indians also valued him foremost as a fundamental source of veteran leadership in the clubhouse. Murray could teach the younger players the right way to conduct themselves and lead by example. He helped mentor Cleveland's up-and-coming hitters with the same type of wisdom that helped him to seven trips to the All-Star Game in an Orioles uniform, including selections every year from 1981–86.

Carlos Baerga remembers Murray doing most of his talking with his bat, but also spending time discussing hitting with Manny Ramírez and Albert

---

[2] Instead, Morris would start in twenty-three games for the '94 club, compiling a 10–6 record with a bloated earned run average of 5.60. He then left the team after a mutual split in August to retire to his ranch in Montana. John Hart later said that it was the end of the line for Jack, but he served his purpose in the Indians' puzzle nonetheless.

Belle. That was what his acquisition was designed to do, John Hart thought. "Eddie's leadership really settled us," Hart recalls.

The second position player Hart signed out of free agency was a bargain deal that brought veteran backstop Tony Peña to Cleveland. The Indians would pay him almost $2 million per year less than his former club, the Boston Red Sox, for a catcher who had also recently won his fourth Gold Glove.[3] Peña would earn $400,000 in 1994, hitting .295 in over forty games as he filled in for the injured Sandy Alomar Jr. This signing proved to be even more valuable, as Peña found himself behind the plate for the majority of the Indians' games in 1995, as well, with Alomar recovering from knee surgery.

As the Indians broke camp at the end of spring training in 1994, the front office was eager to showcase its retooled major-league team, which had been six years in the making. What made the start of the coming season even more special was the extra fanfare Dick Jacobs provided, as promised. The Indians returned from Winter Haven, only to find a brand-new ballpark and a reenergized fan base waiting for them.

---

[3] Peña had won the award three times with the Pittsburgh Pirates in the 1980s and again in 1991 while with the Boston Red Sox. Now the Indians' roster featured great depth behind the plate with the award-winning catchers from '90 and '91.

Chapter Twenty-One

THE HOUSE THAT JACOBS BUILT

John Hart had been concerned when Major League Baseball released the 1994 schedule, which slated the Indians to start the season at home against the dangerous Seattle Mariners.

"We're drawing Seattle," the Indians general manager said. "That means Randy Johnson. You watch and see, he might drop a no-no on us coming right out of the gate."

The 6-foot-10, flame-throwing left-hander was coming off his second of ten All-Star campaigns; bullying Cleveland over nine hitless frames would have been the worst way to debut the Indians' brand new stadium.

On April 4, 1994, the "Big Unit" showed up in typical form, with his mustache, mullet, and a whole lot of moxie. He mowed through the lineup for seven no-hit innings, before Sandy Alomar Jr. reached base on a single to right field in the eighth for the first Indians hit in their new ballpark. Sure enough, the Indians won in walk-off fashion on a single from Wayne Kirby, and Hart breathed a sigh of relief. It was a proud day for the franchise, and the city as well. A sea of fans clad in Wahoo red, white, and blue packed the stands. President Bill Clinton went out to the mound before the game to deliver the ceremonial first pitch and christen the stadium. After the opener, the reporters asked Mike Hargrove what he would miss about the old park.

"You know, I honestly can't think of anything."

But he paused for a moment and reflected. Hargrove had experienced Municipal Stadium in uniform through two contexts; first as a player and then as manager of the ball club. The daily conditions were far from appealing. He could remember coming to the ballpark and immediately wanting to head to the showers because he felt filthy from the moment he walked into the complex. No matter how much cleaning the stadium crew did (and they were out using a pressure washer *all* the time), the place was always dirty. When the midges flew in off the lake and swarmed the ballpark, the conditions were even worse.

Municipal Stadium's homemade batting cages were a far cry from the three indoor hitting areas at the new Jacobs Field. Teammates with allergies sneezed and their eyes watered whenever they took cuts out beneath the center-field bleachers. *They were in trouble*. The hitting surface was nothing more than a layer of dirt and dust. Players and coaches always had to retie the nets because they would rot and fall apart. The old stadium's cages were shorter than the regulation size and the ceiling came lower, making practice an even more dangerous exercise than hitting inside the ancient enclosures at Fenway Park. Charlie Manuel had to be alert whenever he threw batting practice in the cage so he wouldn't get beaten by line drives ricocheting off the walls and abusing his arms and legs. And because the cages were outside, players could only get work in when weather permitted.

The field also left much to be desired. This was one of the pitfalls of sharing a multipurpose sporting facility with the Browns. The groundskeepers were prompted to paint the grass a healthier shade of green and to conceal the cleat markings and football lines each week. As if it wasn't enough for the diamond to double as a gridiron, the playing surface was built over a landfill. In the fifth inning of a game in the 1980s, Hargrove looked around his post at first base and spotted a hole ten feet behind the bag in the grass that hadn't been there for the previous four frames.

"I turned around to check and there was a hole about two feet in diameter and six or eight inches deep that, all of a sudden, appeared and hadn't been there before," he recalls. "That was the only time I ever saw anything like that."

On the other hand, Hargrove had also gotten to see Municipal Stadium reach its full potential, when 72,000 fans crammed into the cavernous park and watched Wayne Garland and the Indians beat the Yankees.

"The fans were excited and the noise almost hurt your ears. I had never experienced anything like that."

But those events were overshadowed by the fact that the club had become a fixture at the bottom of the standings and had league-worst attendance figures.

The manager was even on hand to experience one of the most extreme incidents in baseball history; the infamous ten-cent beer night promotion in 1974, during his rookie year with the Texas Rangers.

Cleveland had averaged close to 8,000 fans per game and enticed some 25,000 to come enjoy eight-ounce brews for ten cents apiece. The Indians were forced to forfeit the game on account of the drunken and unruly supporters. A lady ran onto the field, flashed the dugout from the on-deck circle, and kissed the home-plate umpire. A streaker dashed to second base and a father-and-son tandem mooned the crowd from center field. Then, at the pinnacle of the pandemonium, a wall of inebriated fans charged the infield from their seats.

"You almost felt like Custer on his last stand, completely surrounded by people. And they weren't real happy people, either," Hargrove says, recounting the incident. Somebody pelted the first baseman with an empty gallon jug of Thunderbird. He remembers himself thinking, *They already drank it, jerks.* Things got even worse when hot dogs and spit rained down on him from the stands. The Rangers could have been in physical danger had it not been for the Indians players brandishing Louisville Sluggers and taking the field in defense.

American League President Lee McPhail canceled the Indians' remaining ten-cent beer nights. He condemned the promotion, commenting, "There was no question that beer played a part in the riot. America may need a good five-cent cigar, but it doesn't need ten-cent beer."

So after revisiting twenty years and thousands of innings in that decrepit stadium dubbed "the Mistake by the Lake," Hargrove amended his response.

"The only thing I might miss about it is the fact that I didn't get to blow it up."

The move to Jacobs Field was welcome elsewhere around the organization. The Browns only allotted pitching coach Mark Wiley a cupboard-sized storage closet in the bowels of the stadium to stock equipment for the offseason. And for once, Indians' ownership could actually profit from advertising space.

"You see that scoreboard?" DiBiasio says, motioning to the Daktronics video board beyond the left-field bleachers at since-renamed Progressive Field. (Progressive Auto Insurance bought the stadium's naming rights before the 2008 season.) He starts naming the list of sponsors who bought space to advertise around the 5,364-square-foot screen. It was, for a time, the largest video display of its kind at any sports facility in the world.[1]

There's Sherwin-Williams and Key Bank, Medical Mutual, Budweiser, United Airlines, Drug Mart, Pepsi, Sugardale, Sports Time Ohio and Major League Baseball Tonight, among others. It's an asset the Indians didn't have at Municipal Stadium.

Heck, even the media groaned about the all-metal press box at the old ballpark. It was frigid in April and didn't have heaters. And by the middle of the summer, it became a steam room. Bat giveaway days resulted in a cacophony, when an army of kids at the ballpark banged and splintered their souvenir sticks outside the box. Inside, cobwebs and dead spiders fell from all

---

[1] The Indians installed a new video board before the 2016 season, measuring 13,039 square feet. It remains the largest in Major League Baseball. As of 2018, the largest video board at an American professional sports venue is the 62,350-square-foot Daktronics board at Mercedes-Benz Stadium, home to the Atlanta Falcons.

corners of the room. The only plus-feature was its vantage point. Out over the plate, it was one of the closest spots in Major League Baseball for writers to catch a game. But the box was dangerously close to the action.

"You could get killed by a foul ball if it came roaring up there with your head down writing," the *Plain Dealer's* Paul Hoynes says. "We'd keep the windows open on what looked like big meat hooks and kind of wondered what would happen if a ball came. Might decapitate you. A window shattered one time when a foul ball went through it and covered a Detroit writer in glass."

Aesthetically, Dick Jacobs couldn't have been happier with the job HOK Sport did in designing his retro-modern park, which incorporated similar principles to showcase the Cleveland skyline. From the outside, it appeared to be more of an urban baseball palace than it was a stadium. The exterior featured Atlantic green granite accents, Kasota stone, limestone and brick masonry with exposed structural steel to complement the downtown cityscape. The state-of-the-art illuminated scoreboard and replay screen, the largest freestanding scoreboard display in Major League Baseball, faced the field of play above the left-field bleachers. Toothbrush-shaped light stacks illuminated the park under the night sky. One of the complex's defining characteristics, they were later incorporated into the design for the stadium's logo and signage.

The designers wanted to create an intimate baseball setting, so they set the field below street level. They reduced the seating capacity from 74,438 at Municipal Stadium to 42,865 in the new building. HOK angled all the dark green-painted seats toward home plate, staggered the terraces, enclosed the luxury boxes in clear glass, and kept the concourses open to improve the fan experience. And speaking of fan experience, the facility also featured the open-air Market Pavilion, which more closely resembled Cleveland's West Side Market than the typical concession stand with its variety of dining options. It offered fans a multicultural sampling of foods and beverages emblematic of Cleveland culture, ranging from pierogies and sushi to hot dogs and the hometown delicacy: brown, spicy Bertman original Ball Park Mustard.

In spite of its modern features, the design maintained the traditional, asymmetrical layout of the classic ballparks, with inviting, finely manicured Kentucky Bluegrass. A characteristic touch, a 19-foot wall in left field gave brigades of fans the optimal viewpoint to snag a long ball off the bat of any of the Tribe's sluggers along the Home Run Porch.

All in all, the club's move from the lakefront to 2401 Ontario Street could not have been a more welcomed change.

"It was like going from the outhouse to the penthouse," Indians broadcaster Tom Hamilton says. "Municipal Stadium was the worst baseball facility in America, and you went to one of the elite ballparks in America. You couldn't go in a more diverse direction."

"Just like covering a game in the Taj Mahal," adds Hoynes. "It was like, 'So this is how the other half lives.' First class all the way. You wouldn't believe it could happen in Cleveland."

Fittingly, the planned Cleveland Indians Baseball Park bore the name of the franchise's benefactor when it opened. Dick Jacobs bought the naming rights to the facility, stamping his name on his ballpark and cementing his place in the city's baseball tradition. He provided a new stage upon which the beloved franchise could perform, and the successes that took place in the following string of seasons could not have been scripted.

Jacobs Field Firsts		
Event	**Person**	**Date**
First Pitch	President Bill Clinton to Sandy Alomar Jr.	April 4, 1994
First Hit	Seattle Mariners outfielder Eric Anthony (home run)	April 4, 1994
First Indians Hit	Catcher Sandy Alomar Jr. (single to right field)	April 4, 1994
First Double	Manny Ramírez	April 4, 1994
First Triple	Seattle Mariners outfielder Ken Griffey Jr.	April 7, 1994

First Home Run	Seattle Mariners outfielder Eric Anthony	April 4, 1994
First Indians Home Run	Eddie Murray (career homer No. 442), a seventh-inning solo shot to deep left-center field off Seattle Mariners left-hander John Cummings	April 7, 1994
First Indians Run	Candy Maldonado (on a double by Manny Ramírez)	April 4, 1994
First Winning Pitcher	Indians right-hander Eric Plunk	April 4, 1994
First Save	Kansas City Royals reliever Hipólito Pichardo	April 15, 1994

Chapter Twenty-Two

THE STRIKE YEAR AND WHAT COULD HAVE BEEN

The 1994 baseball season was one of change, and not only for the Cleveland Indians. The Commissioner's office created a third division in the American and National Leagues (the Central Division), which opened play that year. John Hart persuaded Dick Jacobs to move the Indians out of the AL East, where the club had been a mainstay, and into the newly created AL Central.

The general manager pitched it to the owner as a more palatable option for his franchise on all fronts. The change in league alignment meant that Cleveland would no longer have to compete with those teams in the division standings. Before realignment, the Indians competed for a single playoff spot against Toronto Blue Jays, New York Yankees, Milwaukee Brewers, Detroit Tigers, Boston Red Sox, and Baltimore Orioles. The proposed change in the division structure would place the Indians and Brewers in immediate competition with the Chicago White Sox, Kansas City Royals, and Minnesota Twins; three franchises that previously competed in the AL West.[1]

---

[1] After another realignment, the Detroit Tigers moved into the AL Central in 1998, taking the spot of the Milwaukee Brewers, who switched over to the National League. The expansion Tampa Bay Devil Rays then replaced the Tigers in the AL East.

Baseball also introduced a new playoff format, which added postseason berths for the winner of the Central and one wild card team. This ensured the Indians' increased odds of contending for the World Series. From an economic standpoint, the balanced schedule would still bring to town the teams that attracted the better crowds (namely the Red Sox, Yankees, and Blue Jays), which was good for fan attendance figures. As long as the Tribe was winning, Hart knew that the fans would buy into it.

And from the start of the '94 season, that's precisely what they began to do. Amid the excitement of the new stadium, the Indians took the city of Cleveland and the rest of baseball by storm. They wrapped up the month of April tied with the Twins for first place in the Central and a 13–9 record, but the White Sox overtook them for a 2.5 game lead in the division standings by the end of May and were narrowly trailing Boston and Baltimore for the single wild card spot. The Tribe improved their record dramatically over the next month to 44–30, jumping 1.5 games ahead of the White Sox. Leading the way was Albert Belle, who had settled down somewhat and was putting up monster numbers in the heart of the order. Albert carried the offense through the end of June, as he was hitting .371 with 23 homers and 67 runs batted in. His batting average cooled ever so slightly by the All-Star break, down to a .349 clip, which was still 79 points over his career average. He was also taking with him 26 dingers and 78 RBI, a first-half performance that placed him in the top-five among the league's hitters in both statistical categories.

With the divisional race hanging in the balance, it was no coincidence that the White Sox exposed Belle for trying to gain an unfair advantage by using a corked bat. The infamous incident took place during the second game back from the All-Star break, when the Indians were visiting Chicago's Comiskey Park. Belle had homered and driven in a pair of runs in a 6–3 losing effort in the first of a four-game series. The next day, July 15, Sox skipper Gene Lamont decided to use his only allotted bat check with Belle at the plate.

Lamont's staff had suspicions about the integrity of the lumber. It seemed uncharacteristic for Belle, a slugger who was known for his pull power, to blast such an inordinate amount of baseballs deep to the opposite field the way he had been doing in batting practice. Lamont signaled for time during the first inning to challenge the bat, which was subsequently confiscated and taken to the umpires' dressing room. Belle was allowed to remain in the game, but the Indians grew nervous over the ordeal and sought a solution. For those who don't know the story, what came next only added to the incident's notoriety. Knowing the bat was corked, the Indians sent a volunteer, pitcher Jason Grimsley, to replace it with a legal alternative. Grimsley snatched a clean bat from the rack and climbed through an escape hatch in the clubhouse ceiling. He snaked his way through the ducts on his stomach, navigating through the dark system of tunnels with the help of a flashlight he held in his mouth. He dropped into the dressing room, stepping down from atop a refrigerator, and replaced Belle's bat before retreating to the visitors' clubhouse. When umpire Dave Phillips returned to his locker after the Indians' 3–2 victory, he found a bat belonging to Paul Sorrento instead of the one in question.

The ump knew something was amiss. The bat caper riddled baseball, and the league office nearly got the FBI involved to investigate the sheer lunacy that had taken place in what was being called the Indians' "Batgate" scandal. Before that could happen, the original, doctored bat was finally recovered, taken into custody by officials, and sawed in half. The investigation revealed a cork plug that had been added to the barrel, which gave Belle additional bat speed. The league suspended Albert at first for 10 games but reduced the punishment to seven contests after hearing his appeal at the end of the month. Even with Belle out of the order, Cleveland showed no signs of slowing down. Though they were again two back of the White Sox, the Indians maintained a three-game lead over the Red Sox for the wild card, and created more distance when Belle rejoined the team from his suspension, winning three of four games on the road in Boston and Toronto.

By August 10, they were posting a 66–47 record through 113 games, and were now only one game behind the White Sox in the division and the sole owner of the wild card spot. Cleveland had gone a major league-best 40–26 since it first gave up the division lead to Chicago at the end of May, and was poised to leap the Sox in the standings again. Offensively, the Tribe was on a tear, plating 417 runs over that span.

But just when it looked as though the Indians were about to end the franchise's forty-year playoff drought, the players' strike brought Major League Baseball to a standstill with a month and a half left to play.

There had been growing unrest between the players and owners ever since the collusion in the previous decade. Part of the problem was that baseball had no official commissioner since the owners' vote of no confidence forced the previous league head, Fay Vincent, to resign in September of 1992. In his three-year tenure, Vincent saw Major League Baseball labor relations intensify in the wake of the collusion settlements, a dip in television ratings, and an increase in player salaries, all of which came at the displeasure of the owners. With no permanent commissioner, MLB saw the Collective Bargaining Agreement expire in December of 1993. Owners proposed a new deal with a salary cap and broadcast revenue sharing, which they posited would save small-market teams from faltering. Their agreement eliminated player salary arbitration, moved free-agent eligibility from six years to four, and in that case, reserved the owners' rights to keep players at four or five years, as long as they matched other teams' offers. The owners also amended the Basic Agreement, handing the eventual replacement commissioner complete decision power over labor negotiation. Despite the players' strong disapproval, the owners passed their new resolutions in January of 1994.

As a supposed incentive to the players, the owners claimed they would raise average salaries from $1.2 million in 1994 to $2.6 million in 2001. The increased pay was a nice gesture, but Donald Fehr, Executive Director of the Players Association (MLBPA), didn't interpret the rest of the agreement as a favorable arrangement for the players. Fehr rejected the proposal in July of '94, and said that the players would threaten to walk out on the season if they were unable to reach an alternative action. The two sides sat before federal mediators to negotiate labor peace in the weeks that followed, but failed to make any real progress. On August 12, the players induced the eighth work stoppage in MLB history and the second since 1990. Bud

Selig, the acting commissioner since Vincent's resignation (and former owner of the Milwaukee Brewers), went on to cancel the remainder of the season thirty-four days into the stoppage on September 14, calling off the World Series and derailing Cleveland's playoff hopes for yet another year.

As can be imagined, the cancellation of the season was met with plenty of disappointment around baseball. The fans were outraged at both sides, but the players also had to face the consequences of stopping when they did. San Francisco Giants third baseman Matt Williams had 43 home runs at the time of the strike, and with forty-seven games remaining, he was on pace to tie Roger Maris' single-season record of 61. Tony Gwynn, who was hitting .394, lost the opportunity to become the first player since Ted Williams in 1941 to finish the season with a batting average of .400 or better. Frank Thomas was putting together a career year: .353 average, 38 homers, 101 RBI, and the major-league lead in runs, walks, on-base percentage, slugging, and OPS. He was voted AL Most Valuable Player for a second-straight year.

Of the strike, Mariners outfielder Ken Griffey Jr. said, "We picked a bad season to have a good year."

That was especially true in Cleveland.

"We were going to win the World Series that year," states Dennis Martínez. A championship might have been anything but a sure shot, but the Indians had every reason to feel so confident about its playoff chances. With Albert Belle and Co., Cleveland boasted the most powerful lineup in the big leagues. The team was on track to hit 239 home runs, or one long ball short of the all-time single-season mark set by the 1961 Yankees, when Roger Maris eclipsed Babe Ruth's record of 60 homers. The Tribe's offensive dominance didn't stop there; the lineup also topped the major-league leader board in practically every other offensive category, including hits (1,165), runs (679), RBI (647), doubles (240), batting average (.290), slugging (.484), and total bases (1,946).

Dick Jacobs directed that the prices on all items in the team store that commemorated the inaugural season at his new ballpark be reduced by 50 percent, in case any fans wanted to buy mementos from what otherwise could have been the Tribe's magical year.

* * *

As bad as the timing was for the Indians, it could not have been any worse for the Montreal Expos, who led the majors with 74 wins despite having the second-lowest payroll. *Les Expos* were on pace to break the century mark in the win column and set single-season club records in nearly every major offensive statistical category. At that rate, Montreal would have earned the second division title in its franchise history and the first, ironically, since the strike-shortened season of 1981. *That* was a heartbreaker. And although baseball would later manage to bounce back around the league, the game was never the same for Montreal on the other side of the strike. In the decade that followed, the Expos never finished better than eight games out of first place. Stars Larry Walker, Moisés Alou, and Pedro Martínez left town as free agents or via trade, as was the case with Martínez, after he won the American League's Cy Young Award in 1997. In 2002, Expos (and eventual Mets) GM Omar Minaya traded future stars Brandon Phillips, Grady Sizemore, and Cliff Lee (along with Lee Stevens) to Cleveland for Bartolo Colón and Tim Drew, putting the franchise back even further. The Expos changed hands twice, and the team even played a portion of the 2003 season in San Juan, Puerto Rico, before relocating to Washington, D.C., when they became the Nationals in 2005. Before their departure, the Expos unfurled a banner, which read, "1994 *Meilleure Équipe de Baseball* / Best Team in Baseball," commemorating what would have been a historic season had it not been for the labor strike.

* * *

Though the strike stalled Cleveland's first playoff festivities in four decades, the Indians received one minor benefit that came as an inadvertent byproduct: They ultimately became the first franchise in baseball history to trade for a player in exchange for dinner. Steak had never been a part of John Hart's initial offer to the Minnesota Twins for Dave Winfield, a twelve-time All-Star whose experience he hoped would add to the clubhouse dynamic, but when Cleveland and Minnesota had announced the deal at the trade waiver deadline August 31, they agreed to swap Winfield for a "player to be named later." The season ended two weeks later, and no such player was ever named in the swap. Winfield, who by then was the oldest active player in the major leagues (forty-three), never even had a chance to suit up with his new club in 1994. Executives from the Indians and Twins eventually settled the transaction over dinner, with Cleveland's front office picking up the check.

Winfield returned to the Indians as a free agent during spring training following the strike. When he arrived, it was clear that Cleveland was no longer the AL's best-kept secret. By all accounts, the previous season was only a teaser for what the Tribe would have in store in 1995 and beyond.

Chapter Twenty-Three

1995: THE WAIT IS OVER

Two hundred and sixty days would eventually pass from the onset of the strike to the resumption of Major League Baseball in 1995. If Indians players weren't listless at home during an ordinary off-season, this prolonged break surely tried their patience; with each passing day spent staring out of their windows at barren trees and the perpetual gray of northeast Ohio's bleak winter.[1] They were saddled with a mix of anxiety and giddiness, the same conflicting emotions that children experience as they anticipate presents under the Christmas tree; only this lasted every day for almost nine months. The waiting felt like an eternity and it gave them more time to think about how close they had been to achieving the first of what they hoped would turn into annual playoff appearances.

The local fans felt it, too. While other cities scorned baseball during the 1994–95 strike, the fans in Cleveland shared in their players' anticipa-

---

[1] While it is unlikely that all the Indians players lived in the area during the off-season, the team required players to live in and around the city, with many living in the suburbs surrounding Cleveland.

tion. For the first time in four decades, the Indians had managed to create a noticeable air of excitement around town. The fan base had only a taste of it in '94, and it still waited for its beloved Tribe to make a return to postseason play. But Cleveland was going to first have to wait for the end of the strike for that to happen.

February rolled around without the owners and the Major League Baseball Players Association having reached a deal, which prompted union players to hold themselves out of spring training. Instead, replacement players reported to the big-league camps in Arizona's Cactus League and Florida's Grapefruit League in their absence. Some had been retired players, others were minor-leaguers who had not yet been put on 40-man rosters and, as such, were not members of the MLBPA. Replacement teams played essentially meaningless exhibition contests. Teams could carry thirty-two players on the Opening Day roster, twenty-five of whom were eligible to play in games. Owners instituted rules for regulating replacement rosters. They did away with the disabled list, and declared that players could not be placed nor picked up on waivers. They imposed salary limits, too. Base pay was set at $115,000, and players could earn bonuses of up to $10,000 for signing and making the roster. No more than three players per team could make up to $275,000 each.[2]

The strike continued into April, which delayed the start of the regular season. This afforded John Hart additional time to shop the free-agent market for pitching. He didn't wait for the new season to commence before making three deals.

---

[2] Thirty-six replacement players without previous major-league experience eventually reached the big leagues following the strike. Some, including Kevin Millar, Shane Spencer, Damian Miller, and Brendan Donnelly contributed to World Series championships. These players remained eligible for arbitration and league pension after the strike; however, they lost union voting rights and couldn't appear on MLBPA licensed products, due to their participation on replacement teams.

The highest-profile acquisition came on April 8, when Hart signed Orel Hershiser, upgrading the starting rotation. A superstar in his own right, Hershiser had made a name for himself with the Los Angeles Dodgers in 1988, when he paced the National League with 23 wins, 267 innings pitched, and 15 complete games, helping the franchise to its sixth World Series title. "Bulldog," as he was nicknamed by manager Tommy Lasorda, had garnered honors in 1988 when he was named the National League's Cy Young Award winner, World Series MVP, and set the record for most consecutive scoreless innings (59), a record still unbroken as of the date of this book's publication. But that was 1988, and Hershiser had only won a combined twenty-two games in 1992 and 1993 after coming back from reconstructive shoulder surgery. After going 6–6 with a 3.79 ERA in the strike-shortened '94 season, the final year of his three-year, $7.9 million deal, it was clear to the Bulldog that the Dodgers were not likely to bring him back. (Certainly not for the $3.3 million they paid him that year.) That made Hershiser an early target for Hart.[3]

"He was a veteran right-hander, a proven winner that still had ability," Hart says. Hershiser also profiled as a positive addition to the clubhouse dynamic, given his character qualities and competitiveness. Dick Jacobs hosted him to dinner at Johnny's Downtown, an upscale restaurant in the Warehouse District. They ate in the downstairs wine room—a favorite spot of the owner—where he often held court to discuss business and baseball matters. There, Jacobs expressed that Hershiser was the missing piece to help the Indians go all the way. Hart could promise him ample run support; the Indians' lineup boasted 6.01 runs per game in 1994, the highest in the majors.[4] The fans would pack the new ballpark every night, and he would have an opportunity to pitch in meaningful baseball games—in Cleveland,

---

[3] This was the richest three-year contract ever signed, up to that point. He made $11.9 million over the next three years (1992–94).

[4] The second closest were the Yankees, who averaged 5.93 runs per game.

no less.[5] The Indians were able to sell Hershiser on that idea, and he agreed to a one-year, $1.5-million deal.[6]

The signing pumped up fans. Hershiser was an established talent, and he was choosing to come to Cleveland; something fans were still not used to happening.

Two days later, the Indians signed Paul Assenmacher, a crafty left-handed specialist who had made more appearances (283) in the last five years than any other major-league reliever. Assenmacher, thirty-four, had already pitched out of the bullpen for the Braves, Cubs, Yankees, and White Sox, and was entering his tenth season. Whereas the other Indians relievers were power arms, Assenmacher was the type of pitcher who could fool hitters with off-speed and breaking pitches. He provided Mike Hargrove and pitching coach Mark Wiley an alternative to match up against opposing hitters in critical situations.

The final acquisition came at the end of the month in the form of Buddy Black, a left-handed starter, for whom Cleveland had already traded once before in 1988. Black had been a member of the 1985 Royals' championship club, and was now entering his fifteenth and final season, at age thirty-eight.

With the end of the strike nearing, the major-league players returned to Florida for an abbreviated spring training, which lasted about three weeks. And just as they were getting into baseball shape, the teams launched into the regular season. After starting the season on the road (4–3), Cleveland was victorious in their home opener, winning, 5–1, over the Minnesota Twins. Charles Nagy picked up his first "W" of the season, and José Mesa

---

[5] While the Indians were becoming playoff contenders, the Dodgers hadn't made the playoffs since 1991.

[6] Hershiser caught a second wind and ended up staying in Cleveland for three years. He went 45–21 (a .682 winning percentage) with a 4.21 ERA over ninety-one starts. The Bulldog was instrumental down the stretch in 1995: Hershiser went 4–1 in the postseason; he went 2–0 with a 1.29 ERA versus Seattle in the American League Championship Series, en route to being named ALCS MVP.

notched his first save since being converted from the rotation. (More on this in a moment.) Two days later, in finishing up their series with the Twins, the Indians won the longest game in team history, 10–9, in seventeen innings. Cleveland and Minnesota used a combined total of seventeen pitchers during the contest, which dragged on for six hours and thirty-six minutes before Kenny Lofton eked out a walk-off single to center field. Manny Ramírez scored, sending his teammates springing from the dugout to celebrate around home plate. On May 9, the lineup plated eight runs in the first inning before recording an out, all in support of Hershiser, who picked up his first win as a member of the Tribe. The victory moved the Indians into first place in the AL Central, where they remained a fixture for the rest of the year. But in May, the Indians were just getting started.

Chapter Twenty-Four

THE PENNANT RUN

One of the earliest hinge-points of the season took place on May 20 in Boston. The Indians had just plated four runs in the eighth on home runs from Albert Belle and Jim Thome to pull ahead, 7–5, over the Red Sox at Fenway. Mike Hargrove called in Mesa for the save situation in the ninth inning. Mesa quickly retired the first two hitters he faced, but allowed a two-out single to the shortstop, John Valentin. The on-deck hitter was burly slugger Mo Vaughn, a long-ball threat who represented the game's tying run. In the dugout, Hargrove had a choice to make. Paul Assenmacher was already warming in the bullpen; conventional baseball wisdom would have suggested calling upon Assenmacher, the southpaw, to face the left-handed Vaughn.

In five years as a major-league starter, Mesa had but one winning season: 1990, when he went 3–2 in seven starts for the Orioles. Baltimore traded Mesa to Cleveland in 1992, but he failed to find success in the rotation. He moved to the bullpen in 1994, bringing with him a high-90s fastball (for which he earned the nickname "Señor Smoke"), a mid-90s sinker, and a Fu Manchu mustache. All of those qualities made the twenty-nine-year-old from Azua, Dominican Republic, the leading man for the closer's role in 1995.

And during the showdown with Vaughn, Hargrove and pitching coach Mark Wiley decided they would see for themselves whether they could trust Mesa, their otherwise unproven closer, in the ninth inning with the game on the line.

Veteran backstop and fellow countryman Tony Peña trotted out to the mound to help Mesa focus, motioning toward the bullpen to hype him up. "They're going to bring in the lefty," he said. But Mesa had other ideas. He got a called first strike, but proceeded to fall behind in the count, 2–1. Mesa then settled down, pumping two pitches past Vaughn, who waved at and missed the third strike to end the game. In that moment, the Indians knew they had the right man as their closer.

The win in Boston springboarded the Indians, who won two of the next three series and finished the month of May with a 21–9 record. Cleveland created some space atop the division, thereafter, as the Tribe carried a 16–2 stretch into the middle of June, distancing themselves by 7.5 games over the second-place Kansas City Royals. Cleveland's .750 winning percentage (33–11 record) was the highest in baseball. They were six games better than the Red Sox, the next-best team in the American League. A win over the Red Sox on June 20 marked their 102nd win in 162 games (the length of one full regular season) since the opening of Jacobs Field in 1994.[1] That same day, the franchise reached a monumental attendance benchmark, as the millionth fan of the '95 season passed through the turnstiles. To put this into perspective, consider that Cleveland fell short of one million fans for its full-season attendance twenty-five times since the last time it reached the World Series in 1954.

"Somehow the baseball fans have come out," thirty-nine-year-old designated hitter Eddie Murray said. The Indians' recent successes weren't the only draw at the ballpark. By June, the fans were also coming in hopes of witnessing history, as Murray, a nineteen-year veteran, was quickly approaching 3,000

---

[1] The Indians finished the strike-shortened season of 1994 with a record of 66–47. After 162 games (from the start of the '94 season into the '95 season), the Indians had a 102–60 record.

career hits (he came into the season with 2,930). Fans tallied his career total on homemade signs they brought to the stadium, and on June 30 in Minnesota, Murray eventually accomplished the feat, lining a single off the Twins' Mike Trombley in the sixth inning of a 4–1 win, becoming the twentieth man in baseball history to accomplish the feat.

By the middle of July, fans in northeast Ohio weren't alone in recognizing the talented Indians, as Cleveland had taken a major-league best 46–21 record into the All-Star break. Fans across the country voted three Indians to the starting lineup for the American League at the Midsummer Classic in Arlington, Texas: Kenny Lofton, who manager Buck Showalter tabbed as the leadoff hitter; Carlos Baerga, the switch-hitting second baseman, who was the third-hardest man to strike out in baseball; and Albert Belle, who was hitting .312 before the break and had a candy bar named after him.[2] And Belle hadn't even heated up offensively yet. (His 14 home runs and 51 runs batted in were solid totals by everyone's standards except his own.) Belle participated in the Home Run Derby during All-Star weekend, hitting a then-record 16 long-balls before losing in the finals to Frank Thomas of the Chicago White Sox. Joining Lofton, Baerga, and Belle in Arlington were three reserves: right-hander Dennis Martínez (who was 8–0 with a 2.47 ERA to that point); their closer, José Mesa (who had 20 saves); and, for the first time in his career, Manny Ramírez.

At twenty-three years old, Ramírez was enjoying his second full-season in the big leagues. Ramírez had made the club's roster from Opening Day in 1994, and in his rookie campaign, hit for a .269 average, 17 home runs, and

---

[2] It's been said that great sluggers should have candy bars named after them. (If it hasn't been said before, it has been now.) There's a Baby Ruth bar, which actually has no tie to the former Yankee legend. But Reggie Jackson and Ken Griffey Jr. each had their own candy bars named after them, and Belle's agents teamed with Malley's Chocolates to introduce a chocolate-covered crunch bar, the Albert Belle Bar, in 1995. Everyone was excited about the unveiling of the new sweet except for . . . Albert Belle.

60 runs batted in. He also had eight assists from the outfield; a performance good enough for a second-place finish in the voting for AL Rookie of the Year (behind Kansas City first baseman Bob Hamelin, who was out of the game by the time he was thirty). Ramírez came into 1995 and was hitting over .400 until late May. This prompted Showalter to include Ramírez as a reserve for the AL squad, and deservedly so: Ramírez' triple-crown numbers edged even those of Albert Belle.[3]

The National League bettered the American League, 3–2, to win the All-Star Game, but the Indians hitters reached base five times in the exhibition (Baerga went 3–3 in the game and Ramírez walked twice).

The Indians came back from the break and proceeded to win eleven of their next twelve contests (taking seven from the Athletics alone). Manny Ramírez punctuated the first of two sweeps of the A's on the afternoon of Sunday, July 16, in dramatic fashion. The Tribe outfielder took a 2–2 offering from heralded closer Dennis Eckersley deep into the left-field bleachers for a walk-off solo home run in the twelfth inning. As Ramírez trotted around the bases, a television camera panned to Eckersley, who walked away from the mound in disbelief, clearly mouthing the word "Wow!" This would become one of the more memorable images from the Indians' historic '95 season.

While Manny's monstrous home run was definitely a head turner, Albert Belle would join him on the highlight reel two days later.

While the Tribe were the talk of the American League, the California Angels had the second-best record in the league, leading the Rangers by one game in the West. Cleveland had dropped the first of a two-game series to California. Some of the Angels, namely designated hitter Chili Davis, had taken exception to being overshadowed by the Indians in the media. Davis

---

[3] While Ramírez finished his '95 campaign with a .308 batting average, he held his average at .400 until May 28. At age twenty-three, Ramírez was the youngest to ever hold his batting average at or over .400 that late in the season. The youngest before Ramírez was Billy Grabarkewitz, who had his batting average at .402 on May 27, 1970, at the age of twenty-four.

was quoted in the *LA Times*, saying, "They're a good team, but so are we. . . . We've heard a lot of people say, 'You guys have played well, but you haven't played Cleveland yet.' That's unfair to us. We're not saying we're better than Cleveland—they're awesome. But to all the people who doubt us, who think we're a fluke: Shut up; we can play." And on the evening of July 18, the Angels carried a 5–3 lead into the ninth inning before handing the ball over to otherwise dependable closer Lee Smith, the active career saves leader (454 as of July 18), who on this muggy July night in Cleveland was not his typical self.[4]

Smith had pitched the first two months of the 1995 season without surrendering a run (he gave up his first earned run on June 28, in a loss to Texas). At one point during that stretch, he notched his sixteenth consecutive save in as many appearances, breaking the major-league record previously set by Doug Jones with the Indians in 1988.

Once Smith entered the game, Hargrove pinch-hit Wayne Kirby for third baseman Álvaro Espinoza. (Espinoza, a right-handed batter, matched better against starting pitcher Mark Langston, a lefty, than the Indians' everyday third baseman, the left-handed-hitting Jim Thome.) On the second pitch of the at-bat, Kirby bounced a ground ball to first baseman J. T. Snow, who was regarded as one of the best fielders at his position. In this instance, Snow struggled with the hop, allowing Kirby to reach on what was scored an infield hit.[5] Hargrove pinch-hit again, this time swapping Thome for center fielder Rubén Amaro. Thome went down swinging, but Kirby was able to steal second base on the strikeout and get into scoring position. Omar Vizquel followed with a line drive to the hole between third base and shortstop. Angels shortstop Gary Disarcina made a play on the ball, but it ricocheted off the tip of his glove and into left field, allowing Kirby to advance to third base. Smith then unintentionally walked Carlos Baerga on four consecutive pitches, the fourth skipping in the dirt to load the bases. The walk set the stage for Belle, who

---

[4] Smith saved 478 games over his 18-year career, and was later surpassed by Trevor Hoffman (601) and Mariano Rivera (652).

[5] Snow won his first of six consecutive Gold Glove Awards at first base in 1995.

glared menacingly at Smith as he strode toward the plate. That night marked another sellout at the Jake, and the crowd of 41,763 fans rose to its feet, chanting *Al-bert! Al-bert!*

Earlier in his career, Smith intimidated hitters with an overpowering fastball and an unrelenting attitude on the mound. As his age went up and his velocity came down, he had to incorporate a slider to keep hitters off-balance. He remained a daunting opponent—even in the ninth inning—but this time in Cleveland, Smith hung a 1–2 slider out over the plate. Belle smacked it to straightaway center field, and knew it was gone the moment the ball struck his bat. Belle hopped once and watched his towering blast soar into the nighttime sky as he began his trot around the bases, raising his fist before reaching first. It was the second grand slam Smith gave up in '95 (the first was to Mark McGwire on June 30). The fans erupted, the dugout emptied, and the players mobbed Belle at home plate. Belle's walk-off marked the fourteenth come-from-behind victory of the season for the Indians, and this latest installment of late-inning heroics generated momentum to propel the Tribe into the second half of the season.

* * *

With the non-waiver trade deadline approaching toward the end of July, John Hart was in a position unlike any other Indians executive in four decades: Hart could now make a deal to aid the Indians as they prepared for a playoff run. Given their offensive performance (the Tribe led the majors in every offensive category imaginable), Hart targeted another upgrade to his pitching staff, which already could claim the league's lowest earned run average. In his first year in the American League, Orel Hershiser had the league figured out after the All-Star break, going 11–2 in the second half; Charles Nagy posted a 6–1 mark in his last eight starts; and José Mesa was recording saves at a record pace.[6] But Hart knew he could never have too much pitching, so he traded with St.

---

[6] Mesa would finish the season with 46 saves, which would lead the AL and the most in his 19-year career.

Louis for right-hander Ken Hill. For Hill, Hart dealt rookie infielder David Bell, 6-foot-7-inch right-hander Rick Heiserman (a third-round pick in the '94 draft from Creighton University), and farmhand Pepe McNeal. In return, Hill gave the Indians steady pitching down the stretch, tossing 74.2 innings in the final two months of the regular season. Although he fared just a 4–1 record in his eleven starts, Cleveland won ten of the games in which Hill pitched.[7]

During that time frame, the Indians' pitching benefited from even better run support than it had all year. In all, the '95 club scored an average of 5.83 runs per game. Their average run output each night had already exceeded the averages in the respective leagues: 5.07 runs per game in the AL, 4.63 runs in the NL. In August and September, the Tribe's offense accelerated ahead to 6.05 runs per game, or almost a full run better than the other AL and well beyond the NL clubs' averages.

Albert Belle's monster second-half largely facilitated the Tribe's offensive onslaught down the stretch. Belle launched into a home-run binge in August, swatting 16 with 13 doubles in 127 at-bats. His power explosion translated into one homer for every eight at-bats. Belle finished the month in dramatic fashion, hitting walk-off homers on consecutive nights against Toronto.

The first of the game-winners came on August 30, and Belle delivered a two-out shot to deep left-center field off the Blue Jays' Tony Castillo in the bottom of the fourteenth inning. The next night, Jimmy Rodgers replaced Castillo for the Jays in the tenth inning. Rodgers induced a ground ball from Omar Vizquel to shortstop for the first out, but walked the next batter, Jim Thome. Belle followed with a two-run blast, sending another sellout crowd at the Jake home happy.

The fans had been staying at the ballpark into the late innings each night, regardless of the score, because they had grown to expect the Indians to mount dramatic comebacks.

---

[7] Hill started eleven games for Cleveland, in which the team went 9–2, and came in for relief on October 1 (pitching the seventh and eighth innings), in which the Indians were victorious.

"You'd go along, and we'd be losing, 3–1, 4–1, 5–2, and the next thing you know, the seventh inning comes around and it just exploded," Thome says. "We believed in ourselves and, more importantly, we competed."

Carlos Baerga adds, "Never, never, never have I seen anything like that before."

The celebrations got bigger and more extravagant and the season went on. The scrum that encircled home plate got increasingly boisterous, with players high-fiving and slapping teammates' helmets after they plated the winning run. The celebrations carried into the clubhouse.

Orel Hershiser lockered next to Dave Winfield that year. They shared thirty-four years of MLB experience between them, and each had been a part of a championship team. But the two veterans remained amazed by the clutch hitting performances that enabled the '95 Indians to record fifty-one come-from-behind victories, twenty-eight of which were won in the Tribe's final at-bat.

"We'd come in and go, 'These guys don't realize that this just doesn't happen.'" Hershiser said. "We're ruining young guys' careers this year, because they're going to go the rest of their careers, maybe ten or twelve years, and never play on a team that's this good."

Such a thought must have skipped over the rest of the players in the clubhouse. They were too focused on bringing the ball club and the Tribe faithful back to the postseason to stop and notice. One week later, the Indians achieved the first milestone of their '95 playoff run. Helped by a home run from Carlos Baerga, seven strong innings from Charles Nagy, and a 1-2-3 ninth from José Mesa, the Tribe downed the Seattle Mariners, 4–1, in Cleveland, to register their 86th win of the regular season. Never mind that it was the Tribe's eleventh consecutive home-victory, the thirteenth of their last fifteen games, nor that it marked the most wins for the Indians in any season since 1968. Win No. 86 put Cleveland 22.5 games ahead of the Kansas City Royals atop the AL Central with 22 contests remaining. This meant that the Indians had clinched at least a tie with the Royals for the division, and thus were ensured at the very least a playoff berth as the wild card team, per the expanded format. For the first time since the New York Giants swept them in the 1954 World Series, the Cleveland Indians were bound for the postseason. However, the real celebration followed on the next night, September 8, with the Baltimore Orioles visiting Jacobs Field.

Just two days earlier, Cal Ripken Jr. surpassed Lou Gehrig's streak of 2,130 consecutive games played. The O's were trying to launch into a streak of their own, as they headed to Cleveland trailing the Yankees by four games in the AL East. The Indians pulled ahead to a 3–0 lead in the third inning on a sacrifice fly by Omar Vizquel, which scored Sandy Alomar, and a two-run single from Eddie Murray, which plated Kenny Lofton and Carlos Baerga. Orel Hershiser was in control, giving up two runs over 6.2 innings, before handing the ball over to the bullpen. Paul Assenmacher and Julián Tavárez combined for 1.1 innings of scoreless relief, and then José Mesa entered to close the game in the ninth. After Mesa got Ripken to roll one over to Vizquel at shortstop for the first out, the sellout crowd at the Jake took to its feet. Harold Baines, the O's designated hitter, flew out to right field, and the crowd continued to cheer and clap anxiously. Mesa then walked the catcher, Chris Hoiles, for whom Baltimore manager Phil Regan substituted for pinch runner Jeffrey Hammonds. But Mesa settled back in against third baseman Jeff Huson, who had already doubled and driven in a run earlier in the game. This time, though, Huson popped up to the left of third base in foul territory. The cheers from the crowd proceeded to crescendo, as Jim Thome camped underneath Huson's fly ball. After the ball landed safely in the webbing of his mitt, Thome kept his arm extended with his glove held overhead, as if to signal for the ensuing celebration to commence. The Indians were finally winners of the divisional title for the first time in forty-one years. The dugout emptied onto the field, where the players and coaches hugged and high-fived. It hadn't totally set in that they were division winners, but they were going to savor the moment in front of the fans who had supported them as they sought to end their extended playoff drought.

That was especially important to Mike Hargrove. The manager recollected, "A couple of years before the '95 season, I was somewhere and I was talking to this man, and he was telling me how he had been a fan all of his life, and how his dad had taken him to a game back in '59, or the last time the Indians were any good. He was little, itty-bitty, and he remembered going to the ballpark with his dad, and how he became such an Indians fan because the team was doing well and how that time with his dad was real special to him. He said, 'My son is three years old right now, and before he gets too old, I want to be able to do that for him so he will have the same passion and will look back at this time with me as a real special time.' I'll never forget that night, when Jimmy Thome caught the foul ball and we clinched the division title. I'll never forget walking onto the field, how good I felt. I wished so bad that I could find that guy and say, 'Now you've got a chance to do it.'"

Clinching in front of the home crowd was significant for the players, as well.

"We came to the ballpark every day and the fans were unbelievable," Baerga says. "They packed it for so many days. Then we go on the road and they would follow us. We used to feel like we were the Yankees at that time—fans follow the Yankees everywhere. But the way we were playing, we felt like everyone was following the Cleveland Indians because we were something special."

The team shuffled back into the clubhouse, and, a few minutes later, emerged sporting commemorative T-shirts and hats over their uniforms. They brought with them a banner, which proclaimed the Cleveland Indians as the newly crowned AL Central Champions. Players and coaches saluted the fans and paraded with the banner into the outfield grass, before raising it to fly from atop the right corner of the scoreboard. Then, as the banner was being pulled to its post above the stadium, the familiar Garth Brooks song, "The Dance," began to play over the sound system, just like it did in 1993 after the passing of Steve Olin and Tim Crews. The song had been of personal significance to Mike Hargrove, his players, and coaching staff in the wake of the spring training boat accident, and it was their way of honoring the memory of their departed teammates in this moment of triumph.

A rowdier celebration followed when the Indians returned to find the clubhouse layered in plastic tarp. Players yelled, "Come and get it!" as they reached into coolers of champagne and began popping bottles. Montell Jordan's 1995 hip-hop single, "This Is How We Do It," reverberated from a boom box in the room. The Tribe was ready to party. Owner Dick Jacobs, who seldom ventured into the players' quarters, made an exception and joined in the festivities, too. Upon his arrival, Carlos Baerga, Dave Winfield, Tony Peña, Álvaro Espinoza, and Sandy Alomar promptly covered Mr. Jacobs in beer and champagne. They weren't going to deny the owner the chance to soak up his first division championship the way his players did. Wayne Kirby and pitching coach Mark Wiley double-teamed general manager John Hart with more of the bubbly. Even after they finished the champagne, players and coaches ducked during interviews as their teammates tried to pour buckets full of ice water over their heads.

There was no slowing the Indians in the days following their division-clinching victory. In reality, the Tribe's clinching of the Central on September 8 was the second earliest calendar date in baseball history for a team to claim the division crown. The eventual World Series-winning '75 Cincinnati Reds captured their NL West Division title a day earlier, September 7, back when the league was still comprised of two divisions.[8]

As Cleveland pushed onward toward the postseason, Albert Belle continued on a home-run binge of Ruthian proportions. Belle hit 10 home runs in a span of seven days, including five long-balls over two days in Chicago. He finished the month of September with 17 homers, matching Babe Ruth's major-league record for the most in a month. Belle's second-half brought his season total to 50 home runs, establishing a personal best and a new franchise single-season record.[9]

Whereas Belle had left the yard once in every eight at-bats in August, he improved to one homer for every six at-bats in September. That means that for the final month of the 1995 season, Belle's ability to hit home runs exceeded:

---

[8] In today's three-division format, no other team has managed to clinch its division on a date earlier than the '95 Indians.

[9] Belle's claim to the Indians' single-season home run record was broken in 2002, when Jim Thome hit 52.

Top-10 Single-Season Leaders for At-Bats per Home Run

Rank	Player Name	Year	Number of HR	AB/HR
1.	Barry Bonds	2001	73	6.52
2.	Mark McGwire	1998	70	7.27
3.	Mark McGwire	1999	65	8.02
4.	Mark McGwire	1996	52	8.13
5.	Barry Bonds	2004	45	8.29
6.	Babe Ruth	1920	54	8.48
7.	Barry Bonds	2003	45	8.67
8.	Barry Bonds	2002	46	8.76
9.	Babe Ruth	1927	60	9.00
10.	Sammy Sosa	2001	64	9.02

Belle's home-run rate for the '95 season, as a whole, was one in 10.92 at-bats, which today ranks fiftieth in baseball history. Belle, however, managed to do in 1995 what no other hitter had done before. In September, he added another ten doubles to his season line, bringing his total to 52 two-baggers. Accordingly, Belle is the only player to record 50 home runs and 50 doubles in the same season.

* * *

The last day of the regular season fell on October 1, with the Kansas City Royals visiting the Jake. The Indians soundly defeated their division opponents, 17–7, advancing their lead in the Central to a major-league record 30 games. The win was the Tribe's 100 of the season, bringing their record to 100–44. Later, Hargrove remarked, "Imagine what we could have won in 162 games." Should Hargrove's club have played eighteen more games in the regular season consistent with their winning percentage (.649), the Indians may have finished with another twelve victories, at 112–50, surpassing the 1954 Tribe's franchise mark of 111 wins, but falling four short of the 1906 Chicago Cubs and the 2001 Seattle Mariners' major-league record of 116. Hargrove thinks it could have been possible. His team fared 10–3 in shutouts and 29–11 in blowouts. The players came through in high-leverage situations, going 28–14 in one-run games. Hargrove pointed out that the Indians were undefeated in extra-inning games, which accounted for another thirteen victories.

So much of that success stemmed from the club's high-octane offense. The Indians led Major League Baseball in every hitting category, compiling 207 home runs, 840 runs scored, and a .291 team batting average. The lineup created runs at a rate that was 15 percent higher than the league- and park-adjusted average.[10]

Hargrove says that the performance was a testament to Charlie Manuel's work as a hitting coach.

"Charlie's biggest attribute as a hitting coach was that he could make people believe in what he was saying. He would give you that down-home, aw-shucks stuff, but if you knew Charlie real well, you knew how smart he was. He could disarm players with his country humor. And it wasn't a façade, that's really who Charlie was, but he was sly like a fox."

The Indians ranked second in the majors in isolated power (ISO, .188),[11] trailing the Colorado Rockies by one-one-thousandth of a point, despite the

---

[10] wRC+ (weighted Runs Created Plus), which is discussed again later in this book, is a refined version of Runs Created (RC), a statistic developed by Bill James. It aims to measure a player or team's total offensive value in runs. The statistic automatically adjusts for league and park factors, which allows for comparison, say, between the era of Boudreau and the era of Belle.

[11] Isolated power is a sabermetric statistic that is used to measure hitters' raw power. It is derived by subtracting batting average from slugging percentage.

Rockies playing in the thin air at Denver's homer-happy Coors Field.[12] But to Manuel's credit, their strikeout rate (13.5 percent) was the second lowest in all of baseball. This might come as a surprise, given the Indians' identity as a "masher club."

"Thome and Ramírez bought into [Manuel's hitting philosophies] from an early age, and once everybody saw how good they were, they did too," Hargrove said. He added, "One time, I had Ramírez and Thome hitting [in the] eight and nine [spots]. That's partly because of how young they were. But we had Paul Sorrento hitting eighth or ninth with 25 home runs. The only non home-run hitters were Kenny [Lofton] and Omar [Vizquel]." And where Lofton and Vizquel lacked in power, they made up with prowess in the field and on the base paths. They accounted for a combined 83 stolen bases atop the lineup, and each won the Gold Glove Award as the top fielder at his respective position.

Opening Day Lineup, 1995 Statistics

Pos	Name	Age	BA	HR	RBI	OBP	SLG	OPS
CF	Kenny Lofton	28	.310	7	53	.362	.453	.815
SS	Omar Vizquel	28	.266	6	56	.333	.351	.684
2B	Carlos Baerga	26	.314	15	90	.355	.452	.807
LF	Albert Belle	28	.317	*50*	**126**	.401	*.690*	1.091
DH	Eddie Murray	39	.323	21	82	.375	.516	.891
3B	Jim Thome	24	.314	25	73	.438	.558	.996

[12] Coors Field is traditionally regarded as one of the most hitter-friendly parks in MLB due to the altitude (1,600 meters above sea level), which allows the baseball to travel a greater distance in less dense air.

Pos	Name	Age	BA	HR	RBI	OBP	SLG	OPS
RF	Manny Ramírez	23	.308	31	107	.402	.558	.960
1B	Paul Sorrento	29	.235	25	79	.336	.511	.847
C	Tony Peña	38	.262	5	28	.302	.376	.679

AL Leader

MLB Leader

The bevy of offense put the Indians' pitching staff in a favorable position to win games, but Hargrove noted that it would not have been possible without the help of pitching coach Mark Wiley to help pilot the staff.

"If we go through our lives and have more than one or two very, very close friends, then we are very fortunate," Hargrove said. "I'm fortunate that Mark is one of those guys. I respect and admire him. He may be the most creative baseball person I've ever been around, always looking for ways to make his people better."

At the end of the regular season, the staff led the AL with a league-low 3.83 earned-run average and 3.08 walks per nine innings, despite logging more frames than any other team in baseball. José Mesa's 1.12 ERA and 46 saves—38 of which came in consecutive appearances—made the Tribe's bullpen the most dependable in both leagues. (Mesa finished second in the Cy Young Award voting for the best pitcher in baseball; had he won, it would have marked only the eighth time in history that a reliever had won the award.)

"Obviously with Martínez and Hershiser and Nagy, guys like that, you're going to do well," Hargrove said, "but for keeping them focused and on track, handling them, Mark did a tremendous job."

All of this made the manager feel confident about his club's ability to compete in the postseason.

Chapter Twenty-Five

PLAYOFF-BOUND AFTER FORTY-ONE YEARS

American League Division Series

Game 1: October 3, 1995, at Jacobs Field

Rain delayed the start of Cleveland's first playoff game in forty-one years by thirty-nine minutes. When the game started, Roger Clemens pitched three perfect frames for the visiting Red Sox, who took an early 2–0 lead on a home run from John Valentin. The Tribe came back in the sixth inning, when Albert Belle doubled home Vizquel and Baerga to tie the game. Belle advanced to third base on an error by Sox catcher Mike Macfarlane, and subsequently scored on a single by the next hitter, Eddie Murray, to give the Indians a 3–2 advantage. However, the lead was short-lived, as Boston tied the game in the eighth on a solo home run from second baseman Luis Alicea. Then the rain came again, and for another twenty-three minutes, the game was delayed. The two clubs battled back and forth into extra innings, which was familiar territory for the Indians. Boston then went ahead, 4–3, on a home run by third baseman Tim Naehring, but Belle answered back in the bottom half with a solo home run of his own off Rick Aguilera. And just like they had all year, the Indians had another magic moment in the bottom of the thirteenth inning, when Tony Peña smacked a solo shot into the first row of bleachers in left field, giving Cleveland a 5–4 victory and a 1–0 series lead.

Cleveland, 5; Boston, 4

Game 2: October 4, 1995, at Jacobs Field

The motivation after Peña's late-game heroics carried into the next day, as Orel Hershiser threw eight shutout innings of three-hit ball. Omar Vizquel hit a two-run double in the fifth inning, scoring Paul Sorrento and Kenny Lofton. Eddie Murray added a two-run homer in the eighth, and José Mesa threw a perfect ninth inning, as the Indians won the second game of the series, 4–0.

Cleveland, 4; Boston, 0

Game 3: October 6, 1995, at Fenway Park

The ALDS then headed to Boston, where the Indians saw an opportunity to clinch a spot in the League Championship Series by sweeping the Red Sox in the five-game series. The Tribe jumped out to an early lead, scoring three runs over the second and third innings, before blowing the game open with a five-run sixth. Charles Nagy held the Sox to one run over seven innings, and the Indians were victorious by a score of 8–2, clinching the division.

Remarkably, Cleveland's pitchers held Boston sluggers Mo Vaughn and Jose Canseco hitless in the ALDS. Vaughn had hit 39 home runs and drove in 126 runs for the Sox in '95 while maintaining a .300 average, for which he was eventually named the league's MVP. Canseco, too, hit over .300 and accounted for 24 home runs during the regular season. However, the duo went a combined 0-for-27 in the series.

Cleveland, 8; Boston, 2

Although the Indians made quick work of the Red Sox, they still had to wait to see who their opponent would be in the League Championship Series.

* * *

The other division series pitted the Yankees, winners of the AL Wild Card, against the Seattle Mariners, whose second-half surge into the playoffs was one of the finer stories of the '95 season. In mid-August, the Mariners had found themselves trailing the Angels by thirteen games in the AL West, but rallied around the motto, "Refuse to Lose," and wound up going 25–10 in the remaining thirty-five games of the regular season. Combined with California's complete collapse down the stretch, the Mariners willed themselves into a one-game playoff with the Angels to break a first-place tie for the division title. Led by a dominating pitching performance from Randy Johnson, the M's swiftly defeated the Halos, 9–1, to claim the AL West and punch their ticket to the playoffs.

Seattle needed five games to finish the Yankees, with the series coming to a conclusion in an eleven-inning thriller at the Kingdome. Jack McDowell, winner of the 1993 AL Cy Young Award, gave up a bunt single to Mariners second baseman Joey Cora, who then advanced to third base on Ken Griffey Jr.'s single to center field. That's when designated hitter Edgar Martínez forever etched his place into Mariners lore, hitting a two-run double down the left-field line to lift Seattle into the ALCS. The Mariners then rode the momentum from "The Double" into the League Championship Series.

American League Championship Series

Game 1: October 10, 1995, at The Kingdome

It had been predetermined that the winner of the series between the West champion and its opponent would retain home-field advantage in the League Championship Series; accordingly, the series commenced inside Seattle's Kingdome on October 10. More than 57,000 fans turned out for the opening contest. Bob Wolcott, a right-hander whom the Mariners had called up in August, got the nod to start Game 1 and walked the first three batters he faced. Wolcott then settled down, retiring Albert Belle, Eddie Murray, and Jim Thome in order. The Indians were not able to capitalize on the opportunity to take the lead in the first inning, and in the second frame, Mike Blowers hit a two-run homer off Dennis Martínez to give Seattle the lead. The Mariners' never lost the lead in Game 1, winning by a final score of 3–2.

Seattle, 3; Cleveland, 2

Game 2: October 11, 1995, at The Kingdome

The Tribe came back in Game 2, intent on evening the series before it returned to Cleveland. Manny Ramírez led the charge, clubbing four hits—including two home runs. Orel Hershiser looked like the Bulldog again, holding the M's to one run on four hits over eight innings of work. The Indians took Game 2, 5–2, and suddenly the momentum was shifting their way, with the series heading back to Cleveland.

Cleveland, 5; Seattle, 2

Game 3: October 13, 1995, at Jacobs Field

The pitching match-up in Game 3 saw Randy Johnson against Charles Nagy. Seattle outfielder Jay Buhner's solo homer against Nagy had opened the scoring for the Mariners, but when each pitcher left the game after the eighth inning, the two starters had nearly identical lines.

Pitcher	IP	H	R	ER	BB	SO	BF	Pit
Johnson	8	4	2	1	2	6	30	101
Nagy	8	5	2	1	0	6	30	111

Buhner struck again in the top of the eleventh inning, hitting a three-run homer off Eric Plunk with two outs, ultimately deciding the third game of the series in favor of Seattle, 5–2. Worse, it was later revealed that Albert Belle had twisted his right ankle in a failed attempt to get out of the way of a pitch from Norm Charlton in the ninth inning, which would cause him to sit out Game 4. Coach Hargrove would start Wayne Kirby in his place.

Seattle, 5; Cleveland, 2

Game 4: October 14, 1995, at Jacobs Field

Seeking to excite the hometown fans, the team invited actor Charlie Sheen to deliver the first pitch before Game 4 as his *Major League* character, Rick "Wild Thing" Vaughn. The Indians fed off the energy inside Jacobs Field, scoring three runs in the bottom of the first inning on an RBI groundout from Carlos Baerga and a two-run homer from Eddie Murray. Jim Thome created more distance on the scoreboard for Cleveland, adding a two-run shot to left field in the third inning to give the Indians a 6–0 lead against Andy Benes, who was knocked out after only 2.1 innings. That was more than enough support for starter Ken Hill, who threw seven scoreless frames, en route to the Tribe's 7–0 victory, as Cleveland again evened the series.[1]

Cleveland, 7; Seattle, 0

Game 5: October 15, 1995, at Jacobs Field

To try and give the Indians an additional morale boost, Rocky Colavito made his first appearance at Jacobs Field, throwing out the ceremonial first pitch. With the help of Colavito, the Indians took an early lead in the home-half of the first inning, when Eddie Murray drove in Omar Vizquel on a single to right field. This gave the Indians a 1–0 lead, but an RBI-double from Ken Griffey Jr. in the third off Orel Hershiser tied the game. Hershiser then gave up an unearned run in the fifth inning, and the Mariners got ahead, 2–1, when Belle misplayed a ball hit by Griffey to left field, scoring Cora.

---

[1] Following a single by Carlos Baerga, Slider, the Indians' mascot, danced atop the six-foot wall in right field. The mascot then fell from the wall, tearing his ACL and MCL, and hobbled into the Indians' bullpen before being taken to the hospital. The mascot showed up on crutches for Game 5, and received a standing ovation.

However, the Indians came back again in the bottom of the sixth, retaking the lead via a two-run homer from Jim Thome.

The bullpen contributed three innings of scoreless (and hitless) relief, and the highlight of their performance came in the seventh inning. Hargrove called on Paul Assenmacher to pitch to Ken Griffey Jr. with one out and men on the corners. After a pitchout to hold the runners, the crafty left-hander fed Griffey a breaking ball and a fastball away for strikes one and two, before getting Griffey to chase an elevated fastball for strike three. That's normally when Assenmacher's outing would have ended, but Mark Wiley came to the mound to tell him he'd be staying in the game to face Jay Buhner. Assenmacher managed to strike him out as well. Mesa then pitched a 1-2-3 ninth inning, and the Indians won, 3–2, to claim their third victory in the series. The Tribe boarded the plane and headed back to Seattle with an opportunity to clinch a spot in the World Series with a victory in Game 6.

Cleveland, 3; Seattle, 2

Game 6: October 17, 1995, at The Kingdome

The Game 6 match-up featured the teams' two aces: Dennis Martínez and Randy Johnson.

"He was a very intimidating guy," Carlos Baerga recalled. "I faced two guys in the big leagues who really intimidated you. One was Roger Clemens and the other was Randy Johnson, and every time you step up to the plate you knew that it was going to be like David and Goliath in there. He was going to try to kill you, no matter what. He was a tough guy then."

Johnson was in control into the fifth inning, but the Indians were able to grab a 1–0 lead after Álvaro Espinoza made it to second base on an error by Joey Cora and scored on a base hit from Kenny Lofton.

Martínez stifled the Seattle lineup, clinging to a one-run lead. The Mariners scattered four hits over seven innings but failed to muster a run against the right-hander from Nicaragua. Then, in the top of the eighth, the Indians broke open the game. Tony Peña doubled to right field, and Mike Hargrove inserted Rubén Amaro as a pinch runner. That's when Kenny Lofton came to the plate.

"Before the game, we were talking, doing our strategy for how we were going to beat this guy," Baerga said. "We said to Kenny and Omar [Vizquel], 'We want you to start bunting the ball. [It] doesn't matter if it's an out. We want to get this guy off his concentration. We need to get him pissed off or something like that.' When you put Kenny on first base, [Johnson] was going to start getting crazy right away because he knew Kenny was going to steal."

Lofton followed the plan, bunting safely to the pitcher for a base hit with Amaro moving to third base. Lofton continued his strategy with Vizquel at bat, stealing second base on the first pitch. When Johnson's next pitch got away from catcher Dan Wilson, both runners began to move. The ball skipped to the right of Wilson, passed the Indians' on-deck circle, and went all the way to the fence. Amaro scored from third with ease, and Lofton, seeing how far the ball traveled, made a hard turn around third and raced for home plate. Wilson corralled the ball and made a quick throw to Johnson, who covered the base; however, Lofton was already sliding into the plate. As the lanky pitcher received the catcher's throw and turned to apply the tag, the center fielder hopped to the jubilant Indians' dugout, where the entire bench welcomed him with high fives and helmet slaps.

"Nobody does that," Indians announcer Tom Hamilton said, recalling Lofton's run. "At that point, I think you realized this club was going to win the pennant and go to the World Series."

After Vizquel lined out, Baerga further deflated the atmosphere inside the Kingdome, hitting a solo home run to make the score 4–0. José Mesa pitched another scoreless ninth, getting Buhner to ground out to Espinoza, who fired the ball across the diamond from third base to record the final out of the series. The Indians had clinched the American League Pennant, their first since 1954, and were heading back to the World Series.

The club celebrated on the field at the Kingdome in front of Seattle's fans. Indians legend Bob Feller was intent on joining them. Feller had his designated spot in the press box at Jacobs Field, but traveled on his own to Seattle to witness the Indians clinch the pennant. An exuberant Feller vaulted over a railing near the visitors' dugout and dropped seven feet onto the playing surface. Indians PR man Bob DiBiasio was already down on the turf, directing players and team personnel toward various members of the media for post-game interviews, and he watched the following scenario transpire:

Kingdome security guards watched the seventy-six-year-old Feller as he jumped excitedly onto the field. They rushed over to apprehend the white-haired man, wrestled his arms behind his back and pinned him face up against a padded wall along the edge of the field.

"I look over and I run, grab him, yell at the guy, show him my credential, tell him that [guy] who they have ready to put the handcuffs on face up against the wall is Bob Feller, and boy, those two security guards couldn't have been more apologetic," DiBiasio said.

"It was all because Bob loved this franchise, Mike Hargrove, and was proud [of the fact that] we were heading back to the World Series."

Cleveland, 4; Seattle, 0

Chapter Twenty-Six

THE 1995 WORLD SERIES

Cleveland was beaming with pride for the Tribe and looked forward to finally hosting the Fall Classic. Fans greeted the team when they returned to the airport, and the city held a rally on Public Square the eve of the Series. The Indians' counterparts were the Atlanta Braves, who sought redemption for two World Series appearances in 1991 and 1992 that resulted without them winning the championship. But as far as the Clevelanders were concerned, this was their time. There was a good omen: The Indians' last championship in 1948 came against the Braves while they were still located in Boston. Yet, this time, there was a slight difference: These Atlanta Braves led the National League with a 90–54 record. Bobby Cox's club boasted the finest assortment of starting pitching in the majors, with a rotation that featured a dominant trio of Greg Maddux, Tom Glavine, and John Smoltz.

Maddux, twenty-nine, posted a 19–2 record and exhibited exceptional control. Over 209.2 innings of work, the right-hander tallied 181 strikeouts to 23 walks, and kept his earned-run average to a miniscule 1.63, en route to being named the unanimous winner of the NL Cy Young Award.

Glavine, an athletic six-footer who threw from the left side, recorded a 16–7 record by mixing fastballs, changeups, and sliders in and out of the strike zone to fool hitters. Smoltz, the No. 3 starter, had an arsenal of pitches at his disposal, including a devastating split-finger fastball and slider that allowed him to challenge hitters. Even the fourth man in the rotation, Steve Avery, a 6-foot-4 left-hander, would be a challenge.[1]

Although the Braves had offensive firepower of their own—make no mistake about it—the '95 World Series would be a test between baseball's superior pitching staff and the game's offensive juggernaut.

"We were facing the best four pitchers maybe in the National League that year," Baerga recalls. "It was going to be hard to face a team like that. They were different kinds of pitchers. When we faced Greg Maddux, he doesn't throw hard, but he treated you with the breaking ball outside and came back with the fastball inside. You had to study a guy like that. It was tougher to hit against a Randy Johnson because he throws so hard, but Maddux could get you out easier. Glavine got the outside corner every time, and as soon as you adjusted to go and get that ball, he'd go inside. Smoltz had the nasty slider and a good fastball, too. Everyone wondered if they would stop our hitting."

World Series

Game 1: October 21, 1995, at Atlanta-Fulton County Stadium

The opening matchup featured Maddux against Hershiser, two pitching heavyweights, each of whom had a Cy Young Award to his name. In the first inning, Kenny Lofton reached on an error and stole second and third base before scoring on a groundout by Carlos Baerga to open the scoring, and first baseman Fred McGriff blasted a home run off of Hershiser in the second to tie the game. The Indians got into trouble in the seventh, with Hershiser, Assenmacher, and Tavárez loading the bases and giving up a pair

---

[1] Avery only went 7–13 during the season with an earned-run average of 4.67.

of runs. Maddux didn't disappoint the home crowd, allowing two unearned runs and two hits over nine innings to win his first-ever appearance in the World Series, 3–2.

Atlanta, 3; Cleveland, 2

Game 2: October 22, 1995, at Atlanta-Fulton County Stadium

The Braves turned to Glavine in game two, and once again, the Indians were able to score first, plating two runs in the second inning on a two-run home run from Eddie Murray. Atlanta, in turn, answered back in the bottom of the third. A sacrifice fly from third baseman Chipper Jones and an RBI single from right fielder David Justice tied the contest at two runs apiece. There the score remained until the bottom of the sixth, when catcher Javy López smacked a two-run homer to give the Braves a 4–2 lead. Cleveland narrowed the lead in the seventh, with Lofton reaching base on a single, stealing his way into scoring position, and scoring on an error by Mike Deveraux in left field. The Tribe tried to spark some late-game heroics, which they'd mastered during the regular season, but López picked off Manny Ramírez at first base in the eighth to effectively kill another Cleveland rally. Braves closer Mark Wohlers came in with two outs in the eighth and closed out the game, picking up the four-out save. With that, Atlanta had a two-game advantage before the Series moved to Cleveland.

Atlanta, 4; Cleveland, 3

Game 3: October 24, 1995, at Jacobs Field

The Braves might have felt like they had the advantage in the Series, but the Indians felt the upside in bringing it home to Cleveland.

"We knew what it meant to the city," Hargrove said. His ball club was really looking forward to coming home. The Indians hadn't played a game at Jacobs Field in almost ten days, and apart from the pennant victory in Seattle, the road had not been kind to the Tribe over that stretch.

Cleveland jumped on John Smoltz early, plating four runs to force him out of the game after 2.1 innings. Cox had to turn to his bullpen early and the Indians were able to take a 5–3 lead into the eighth inning. However, a trio of hits and a costly error by Baerga allowed the Braves to pull ahead, 6–5. Alomar doubled home Ramírez in the bottom-half of the inning to tie the game at six, and José Mesa held the Braves at bay for three innings. In typical late-inning fashion, the Tribe got their clutch hits in the eleventh inning. Alejandro Peña replaced Mark Wohlers to start the eleventh, and Baerga redeemed his earlier error with a leadoff double. Baerga was then replaced by the pinch runner Álvaro Espinoza.[2]

After walking Belle, Peña gave up a line-drive single to center field by Eddie Murray. Espinoza scored from second, sealing the Tribe's first victory in the Series.

Cleveland, 7; Atlanta, 6

Game 4: October 25, 1995, at Jacobs Field

With a chance to even the Series, the Tribe turned to Bob Feller for extra luck. The Hall of Famer threw out the ceremonial first pitch prior to Game 4 and received a warm ovation from the crowd. There had been talk of Bobby Cox starting Greg Maddux again in this game, but the manager decided to rest his ace, and instead handed the ball to Steve Avery. Hargrove went with Ken Hill, and the two starters shut out the opposing lineups through the first five innings of play. Twenty-four-year-old outfielder Ryan Klesko put the Braves on the board in the top of the sixth inning with a solo shot, to which the Indians answered with a solo homer from Albert Belle in the bottom-half of the inning. Atlanta pulled ahead after a three-run seventh, and tacked on one more run in the ninth. The Indians weren't able to close the gap in the bottom of the ninth, as they normally had, and lost the game, 5–2.

Atlanta, 5; Cleveland, 2

---

[2] Baerga had accidentally stepped on the plate while swinging in the first game of the Seattle series and twisted his ankle. The pain lingered throughout the playoffs, and eventually cost him the first part of spring training the following year.

Game 5: October 26, 1995, at Jacobs Field

Facing elimination, the last pitcher the Indians wanted to deal with was Greg Maddux. However, Albert Belle hit a towering two-run homer in the first inning—his second of the Series and fourth of the playoffs—to send a message to the Braves: They were not going to have a champagne party today. Orel Hershiser held Atlanta to two runs (one earned) over eight innings, while striking out six. While the Braves tied up the game with runs in the fourth and fifth, the Indians scored twice more against Maddux in the sixth, going ahead, 4–2. Jim Thome tacked on one more run in the eighth inning, hitting a solo shot (his first of the Series and fourth of the playoffs) to put the Tribe ahead, 5–2. It's a good thing that he did, because Klesko homered for a third time in three consecutive games (a World Series record), reducing the Indians' lead to one run. Yet, the Indians managed to hang on, with José Mesa earning his first Series save.

Now, the Indians' only hope was to win in Atlanta to keep their title hopes alive.

Cleveland, 5; Atlanta, 4

* * *

David Justice stirred controversy before the sixth game of the World Series. After seeing the outpouring of fan support that the Indians received in Cleveland, the Braves' outfielder commented to the media that he didn't feel the Atlanta fans were supporting the team with as much intensity as they had during their run to the Series in '91. It was somewhat true; the fan bases of many teams remained somewhat disenchanted in the fallout from the players' strike in '94. From an attendance perspective, the '95 Braves actually averaged close to ten thousand more fans per game than they had in '91. But the headline in the *Atlanta Journal-Constitution* on the morning of Game 6 read "Justice takes a rip at Braves fans."

Justice later defended his comments and asked fans to prove him wrong. With the Braves on the verge of clinching a Series title, this controversy made for a major storyline heading into Game 6.

Game 6: October 28, 1995, at Atlanta-Fulton County Stadium

In the wake of Justice's comments, ABC television broadcaster Bob Costas said in the pregame coverage of Game 6, "Cleveland was one of the few cities that seemed to be immune to the malaise that engulfed baseball elsewhere this year: a beautiful new ballpark, a contending team for the first time in ages. But in Atlanta, like a lot of other places, the interest and, eventually, the passion came back only over time."

The passion was on display that night in Atlanta. Justice was booed heavily during pregame introductions, and the crowd was more energized than it had been in the previous two World Series games there. Cleveland, on the other hand, was trying to become one of only five teams to recover from a 3–1 series deficit in a seven-game series. The others included: the Pittsburgh Pirates (1925, 1979); the New York Yankees (1958); the Detroit Tigers (1968); and the Kansas City Royals (1985).[3] The Tribe was up against Tom Glavine, who forced hitters to chase off the plate with his changeup and jammed them inside with his fastball. That had been an effective strategy for Glavine in Game 2, and it continued to frustrate the Indians in Game 6.

There had been talk that the Braves' pitchers had an unfair advantage with the umpires awarding them a larger strike zone, the effect of which "forced" the Indians to swing at pitches off the plate.

"That was a difference between Atlanta and everybody else—their rotation, and the fact that their strike zone was about four or five inches wider than anybody else's," Mike Hargrove said. "Not trying to take anything away from them, because they had tremendous stuff and the ability to hit their spots consistently like they did, but they didn't throw many pitches on the plate."

---

[3] The Boston Americans overcame a 3–1 game deficit over the Pittsburgh Pirates to win the 1903 World Series, but this was a best-of-nine series. They won the Series, five games to three.

Charlie Manuel spoke similarly about the issue.

"The talk about the strike zone, the more I look about it, to some degree it's correct," he said, recalling his time at the helm for the Philadelphia Phillies in the 2000s. "I felt like that against the Yankees in 2009. We got behind in games with three or four innings left and tried to do too much. Guys swing out of the zone, and it helps pitchers because you feel like you have to. During the year, you just play the game. Against Glavine, the first three or four innings we hit some balls hard at people, and he walked us off the plate and we chased. It's not to say that we panicked, but we tried too hard. There's this sense of urgency that's coming, that you have to do it. You have to do it because you want to, not because you have to. In the playoffs and the World Series, it becomes a have-to situation and guys lose focus."

Glavine was dialed in for Game 6. He went eight innings, only giving up a single to Tony Peña on a weak-hit fly ball in the sixth inning. His performance marked only the fifth one-hitter in World Series history. Despite not having his best stuff, Martínez went 4.2 innings without giving up a run. He struggled with his control, giving up five walks and four hits. As his pitch count got higher (82 in the fifth), Hargrove decided to lift Martínez from the game and turn the game over to the bullpen. The relievers only allowed two hits over the remaining 3.1 innings; unfortunately, Jim Poole allowed one of those to be a solo homer off the bat of the local villain, David Justice.

Mark Wohlers entered the game in the top of the ninth and got Kenny Lofton to pop out to short and Paul Sorrento, who pinch-hit for Omar Vizquel, flied out to center. Wohlers then recorded the final out of the game—and the Series—getting Carlos Baerga to fly to the center fielder, Marquis Grissom. The Indians could only watch in shock from the visitors' dugout as the Braves dog-piled on the infield grass, celebrating Atlanta's first major professional championship. They watched as Bud Selig, then the Executive Committee Chairman for Major League Baseball, presented the Commissioner's Trophy to the Braves, who were now off the hook for failing to win the title in their two previous trips to the World Series.

The Indians, on the other hand, felt defeated. They had come close to delivering the city of Cleveland its first major championship since the Browns in 1964. The stacked lineup was supposed to have enough weapons to carry the Tribe and its fans to a title as it had all year. But in the World Series, superior hitting was bettered by superior pitching. Whereas the Indians hit .291 in the regular season, they hit a dismal .179 as a team against the Braves. And just like that, their magical run was officially over.

Atlanta, 1; Cleveland, 0

Chapter Twenty-Seven

CHANGING EXPECTATIONS AND GETTING BACK

Bob DiBiasio, the head of the Indians' public relations department, had been in contact with Cleveland city officials immediately following the Indians' defeat in the World Series. The city wanted to throw a parade and host a rally. The Indians didn't like the idea of a parade, as they hadn't won and were intent on getting back into position to win the city its elusive championship.

"We didn't win. We didn't deserve a parade or a rally. We were going to get back there and win this thing," DiBiasio said. At the same time, he knew 1995 was a unique year in the franchise's history. His mother had been pregnant with him during the Tribe's last World Series appearance in 1954. He'd never seen the Indians in the postseason in his entire lifetime until that point. "And all of my generation and those who followed, those who begged to at least see a World Series game in their lifetime . . . all of a sudden we were there. It was one of the most cool, communal, emotional experiences you could have imagined, being a native Clevelander, being on the inside, that our franchise was finally able to bring that kind of joy to the community." He decided that it would be important for the players to see and feel that as well. "There was such an outpouring of support for this franchise and these players. It's important for these players of ours to see, even though you lost, what this town thought of you and how much they love and embrace you. This was good for the players that they remember something incredibly positive out of this season, that even though it didn't end up the way we wanted, that people were just thankful for the ride."

So the team officials told the players, upon their return to Cleveland, that there was something special waiting for them. The city and fans still paraded in the streets, but the team boarded a bus from Jacobs Field to Public Square, got on stage, and had a chance to personally thank more than 50,000 fans who turned out to greet them.

"We were all really surprised by it," Mike Hargrove said. "It was a little bittersweet. It made you feel very humbled that people reacted that way to just the fact that we got to the World Series. It sure made you appreciate Cleveland, the people, the fans of the Indians and made you really want to bring a winner here."

DiBiasio needed a player to get on the microphone to address the fan base. The clubhouse dynamic all year had been that of a comedy club; it was a room full of pranksters. Álvaro Espinoza and Wayne Kirby were two of the ringleaders in the mischief, pulling such stunts as planting sticky pieces of bubblegum inside players' hats. On plane rides, they dripped water on Omar Vizquel's head to keep him from sleeping. Other times, Kirby would get to the clubhouse early to hide Albert Belle's bats. "Albert would come to the ballpark and he'd look through his locker. He could tell something was missing, so he would get pissed off and everybody was laughing," Baerga remembers.

Although Espinoza and Kirby masterminded the pranks, it was Vizquel who was acknowledged as the team comedian.

"Omar was like everybody's little brother. He didn't always have something to say, but any time he opened his mouth, the stuff that came out was hilarious," Hargrove says.

DiBiasio approached the Tribe shortstop and told him that he'd been picked to represent the players and talk to the fans. "They love you with a passion," he said.

"What am I gonna say?" Vizquel asked, but quickly continued, "All right, I know what to do."

He got on stage and rolled into a standup comedy routine of sorts, telling his story about being mistaken for Braves second baseman Mark Lemke at an Atlanta shopping mall. He and his teammates thanked the fans and promised to bring them a winner.

That more than fifty thousand fans skipped work and school to greet the baseball team downtown is symbolic of a significant paradigm shift in the Cleveland sports landscape. The status quo that the Indians were perennial losers had just been upended and changed for good. The fans fed off the players' proclamations for a championship the following year and expected them to come through on their word. Both the franchise and the city had finally rejected the culture of losing that had plagued the two for so many years. The fans responded in a remarkable way: The Indians sold out the entire 1996 season before Opening Day.

* * *

Before the start of the '96 season, John Hart made two offseason moves, in particular, that would serve to help his roster toward another run at the World Series. The Indians signed Julio Franco to fill the void left at first base by Paul Sorrento, who elected to become a free agent and signed with the Mariners. Franco, thirty-seven, had won the first baseman's Silver Slugger Award (given to the top offensive player at each position) with the Chicago White Sox before the strike in 1994. He signed to play in Japan during the stoppage, earning the equivalent of a Gold Glove for the Chiba Lotte Marines of the Pacific League. Upon joining the Indians, Franco hit .322 and drove in 76 runs over 112 games, despite missing 49 games due to a recurring hamstring injury.

Hart also added free-agent pitcher Jack McDowell, who took the place of Ken Hill in the rotation. The Texas Rangers had taken note of Hill's performance down the stretch for the Indians, and signed him that offseason. McDowell would go on to log 192 innings and win 13 games for the Tribe.

The 1996 season, in many respects, looked like a continuation of the Tribe's campaign the previous year, with the offense again performing at a high level. With 148 RBI, Albert Belle plated more runs than anyone in baseball, and his 48 homers ranked fourth between both leagues. Jim Thome (38 home runs, 116 RBI) and Manny Ramírez (33 home runs, 112 RBI) also flourished.

Before the trade deadline, Hart made the decision to send Baerga, Espinoza, and cash to the New York Mets. Baerga had been hampered by a string of injuries, which started when he hurt his ankle in the '95 ALCS. He had a down year, hitting .267 with 10 home runs and 55 RBI at the time of the exchange. In return, the Indians got Jeff Kent, the Mets' starting third baseman, and José Vizcaíno, their starting second baseman. The trade gave the Indians flexibility in the field, and for the second year in a row, the Tribe owned the best record in the majors at the season's end, winning 99 games and their second consecutive American League Central title.

The wheels fell off shortly thereafter. In the Division Series, the Tribe drew the Orioles, winners of the Wild Card, whose playoff seed was predetermined to have home-field advantage in Major League Baseball's old, highly unpopular system. The O's quickly took the first two games of the five-game series before it headed to Cleveland. The Indians won the first game at Jacobs Field, but their rally was cut short by Orioles second baseman Roberto Alomar, who hit a solo home run off José Mesa in the twelfth inning of Game 4, stunning the Indians in their home ballpark. They were unable to answer back in the bottom of the twelfth, and fell in the first round, three games to one.

Despite this early elimination, the fans remained unwavering with their expectations for the ball club. The 1997 season sold out before Opening Day, despite a flurry of offseason moves to reshape the Tribe. The series of transactions stemmed from Albert Belle rejecting the Indians' proposed contract extension in April of '96. Belle turned down a five-year deal worth $43 million. The left fielder stood to earn $8.6 million annually, which would have put him ahead of Ken Griffey Jr. as the highest-paid player in baseball.[1] Belle elected to pursue free agency after the disappointing conclusion of the season.

On November 13, Hart negotiated a deal with the San Francisco Giants to bring third baseman Matt Williams to Cleveland. Williams was a former NL home run champion, as well as a three-time Gold Glove and Silver Slugger award winner. He was a defensive upgrade over Jim Thome, who was blossoming into one of the premier power hitters in the AL and better served the Indians at first base. Hart's initial package of players sent to the Bay Area included Jeff Kent, José Vizcaíno, and reliever Julián Tavárez.[2]

A week later, Belle signed a record five-year, $55 million deal to join the Chicago White Sox. His agent negotiated a stipulation in his contract, allowing Belle to immediately become a free agent if his annual pay dropped out of the top three in baseball. Jerry Reinsdorf, owner of the White Sox and the NBA's Chicago Bulls, now had under his teams' control the highest-paid players in two of the four major sports, the other being Michael Jordan.

With Vizcaíno in San Francisco, Hart needed to find a second baseman. Instead, he found a slick-fielding shortstop willing to move to the other side of the infield. Tony Fernández had starred for the Toronto Blue Jays in the eighties, winning four consecutive Gold Glove awards. Toronto traded him to San Diego for Roberto Alomar at one point, but he returned as a free agent in 1993. A switch-hitter, he drove in nine runs during the World Series, establishing a record for a shortstop and helping the Blue Jays to their second championship in as many years. Fernández missed taking part in the '96 Yankees championship run due to a broken right elbow sustained during spring training. Had he been healthy, the Yankees would have moved Fernández around to second base to make room for rookie shortstop Derek

---

[1] Griffey signed a four-year extension with the Mariners after the 1995 season, which paid him $8.5 million annually.

[2] The two clubs completed the deal a month later, with the Indians sending right-hander Joe Roa in return for journeyman outfielder Trenidad Hubbard.

Jeter. Fernández was still on the market in December and held the major-league record for career fielding percentage (.980), which made him an attractive option to complete a formidable double-play tandem with Omar Vizquel. Coming to Cleveland also meant a chance to contend with the Indians, and so he agreed to a one-year deal toward the end of the month.

The sting from Belle's departure had also carried over to affect the Indians' dealings with Kenny Lofton, who had one year remaining on his contract. Lofton was coming off a year in which he hit .317, drove in 67 runs, and tallied a career-high 75 steals. The front office anticipated having to offer him an enormous extension similar to Belle's, in order to retain the center fielder. Fearing that he, too, would depart as a free agent, Hart made the difficult decision to trade Lofton and pitcher Alan Embree to Atlanta, of all places, in the last week of spring training. The Indians received Marquis Grissom, a marquee lead-off man and center fielder, and David Justice, a long-ball threat who would hit for power in Belle's absence. Ironically, both players played a role in Cleveland's World Series demise just two years earlier. (Justice's home run in Game 6 gave the Braves the lead in the final game, and Grissom caught the ball for the final out.) The trade sent shockwaves around baseball.

"This is a trade of enormous magnitude for two very, very good franchises," Hart told the media. "We're talking about franchise-type players."

Both the Indians and Lofton were sorry to be splitting. Lofton was a former Rookie of the Year, and a winner of four consecutive Gold Gloves and five stolen base titles running. "It's painful in the respect that I think baseball in the nineties is extremely apparent in this trade," Hart said. "For both teams, not just the Indians."

The Braves might have lost two players from their championship roster, but they stood to gain in making the trade. In 1997, Grissom and Justice stood to make almost $11 million; Lofton was due to make $4.75 million. This would significantly reduce the luxury taxes they would pay for keeping their payroll around $62 million. Furthermore, Atlanta would no longer be responsible for about $22 million in salary. This was especially relevant, because it gave general manager John Schuerholz the flexibility to extend the contracts of pitchers Tom Glavine and Greg Maddux. Glavine signed a four-year, $34 million extension in May to become the highest-paid pitcher in baseball. Maddux surpassed his teammate in August, signing for five years and $57.5 million.

When the Indians took to the field in April, there were more new players than ones returning from the pennant-winning squad.

C	Sandy Alomar
1B	Jim Thome
2B	*Tony Fernández*
3B	*Matt Williams*
SS	Omar Vizquel
LF	Brian Giles[3]/*David Justice*
CF	*Marquis Grissom*
RF	Manny Ramírez
DH	*David Justice/Julio Franco*

The new-look Tribe went 44–36 in the first half of the '96 season, maintaining a 3.5-game lead over the White Sox atop the AL Central at the All-Star break. This time, Cleveland was on display for the rest of Major League Baseball, as the Indians hosted the 68th Midsummer Classic at Jacobs Field. With the Indians having sold out every All-Star-related event, Commissioner Bud Selig remarked that Dick Jacobs' Cleveland franchise was one of Major League Baseball's crown jewels. If only the previous owner, Steve O'Neill, and Jacobs' brother, David, were still around to hear that.

Justice was the only Indian elected to start for the AL. Former Indian Kenny Lofton was an elected starter for the NL and received a loud ovation from the local fans during pregame introductions, though he was injured and could not play in the game. Conversely, Albert Belle, a reserve, was announced to a chorus of boos.

---

[3] Cleveland drafted Giles in 1989, and he was a September call-up in 1995.

The Indians were also represented by Sandy Alomar Jr. and Jim Thome. Alomar delivered a two-run homer in the seventh inning, which won the game for the AL, and subsequently was named the game's Most Valuable Player.

The Tribe went 42–39 in the second half of the season, clinching their third-straight division title in the process. With two years of prior playoff experience, Mike Hargrove and his team remained poised to reach the World Series for the second time in three seasons. But in order to get there, the Indians would first have to get through the defending champion New York Yankees in the American League Division Series.

Cleveland and New York battled back and forth, taking a seesaw ALDS the maximum five games.

American League Division Series

Game 1: September 30, at Yankee Stadium

The Bronx Bombers mounted a five-run comeback in the sixth inning, helped by back-to-back-to-back home runs from Tim Raines, Derek Jeter, and Paul O'Neill.[4] Mariano Rivera finished the Indians in the ninth inning, and the Yankees won, 8–6.

Yankees, 8; Indians, 6

Game 2: October 2, at Yankee Stadium

Rookie Jaret Wright started for the Tribe opposite Andy Pettitte and allowed the Yankees to get ahead by three runs in the first inning. But Wright, who began the year in Double-A, cruised for another five scoreless innings, long enough for the Tribe to rally back. Cleveland plated five runs in the fourth inning, and Matt Williams added a two-run homer

---

[4] The first two home runs were off Eric Plunk, while the third was off reliever Paul Assenmacher.

in the fifth, helping Wright to his first career postseason victory and the Indians' first of the series, 7–5.

Indians, 7; Yankees, 5

Game 3: October 4, at Jacobs Field

Game 3 had David Wells matched against Charles Nagy. New York took the lead in the first inning, with Raines scoring on an error by Nagy. Williams tied the game in the bottom of the second, scoring on a force play, but the lead didn't last. In the top of the third, Jeter led off the inning with a walk, then stole second and scored on an RBI-single by first baseman Tino Martinez. The Yankees padded Wells' lead in the fourth, when O'Neill smacked a grand slam off of Nagy to effectively silence the crowd inside Jacobs Field. Wells stymied the Indians lineup for the remainder of the night. Cleveland scattered five hits off Wells, who won, 6–1, in a complete-game effort.

Yankees, 6; Indians, 1

Game 4: October 5, at Jacobs Field

Facing elimination, the Indians turned to Orel Hershiser, who faced another veteran, Dwight Gooden, in Game 4. Again, the Yankees managed to get ahead to an early lead, scoring twice in the first inning on an RBI-double from O'Neill and a single by Cecil Fielder. A solo homer from David Justice cut the Yankees' lead to one run in the second inning. Hershiser didn't surrender another run, pitching seven innings, but Cleveland still trailed 2–1 when Mariano Rivera entered the game with one out in the eighth inning. Rivera was appearing in only the second postseason save opportunity of his career since having taken over the full-time closer's role for the Yankees in '97. He got Williams, the first batter he faced, to fly out to right field. Sandy Alomar came to the plate with two outs, and hit a game-tying homer off baseball's eventual career saves leader.[5] In comeback fashion

---

[5] This was a rarity; as Rivera didn't blow another playoff save until 2001.

reminiscent to the '95 season, the Tribe won the game on a ninth-inning walk-off single by Omar Vizquel off Ramiro Mendoza, scoring Marquis Grissom. And all of a sudden, the momentum in the series was returning to the Indians.

Indians, 3; Yankees, 2

Game 5: October 6, at Jacobs Field

Hargrove went back to Wright to start the pivotal fifth game against Pettitte. The Tribe led, 3–0, after a ground-rule double by Ramírez and a single by Williams in the third inning. Fernández drove home Alomar on a sacrifice fly to right field in the fourth inning, giving Wright a 4–0 lead. That was exactly what the rookie needed, as the Yankees scored three runs over the fifth and sixth innings, narrowing Wright's lead to one. Hargrove then handed the game over to his bullpen, which didn't surrender another run. Mike Jackson and Paul Assenmacher only allowed one base runner in two innings of relief, and José Mesa recorded a five-out save, sending the Indians to the American League Championship Series.

Cleveland was to face the Baltimore Orioles in the ALCS; the same team that had eliminated them the previous year in the Division Series. Led by manager Davey Johnson, Baltimore had won 98 games, edging the Yankees by two games for the AL East crown during the regular season. The O's had been awarded home-field advantage, and the ALCS opened at Camden Yards.

Indians, 4; Yankees, 3

American League Championship Series

Game 1: October 8, at Orioles Park at Camden Yards

Brady Anderson set the tone for the AL East champs in Game 1. Anderson scaled the seven-foot wall in center field, taking back a would-be home run from Manny Ramírez to end the first inning. He then led off in the bottom of the frame, hitting a first-pitch curveball from Chad Ogea into the right-field seats. Roberto Alomar, brother of Indians catcher Sandy Alomar Jr., hit a two-run homer to extend the Orioles' lead to three runs in the third inning.

Cleveland only managed to scatter four singles off Baltimore starter Scott Erickson over four innings, and couldn't muster any offense against closer Randy Myers, ultimately losing 3–0.

Orioles, 3; Indians, 0

Game 2: October 9, at Orioles Park at Camden Yards

The Indians scored two runs via a first-inning home run by Ramírez in support of Game 2 starter Charles Nagy. The lead vanished in the bottom of the second, when Cal Ripken Jr. hit a two-run homer of his own, scoring Rafael Palmeiro. Baltimore then pulled ahead on a two-run single by Mike Bordick in the sixth inning, giving the O's a 4–2 lead. Hargrove lifted Nagy from the game and turned to his bullpen, which contributed scoreless relief for the final three frames. Then in typical Indians fashion, the Tribe stunned the Orioles in the bottom of the eighth, when Marquis Grissom blasted a three-run homer to re-establish the Indians' lead at 5–4.[6] Mesa picked up the save in the ninth inning, and the series was even as it headed to Cleveland for three games.

Indians, 5; Orioles, 4

Game 3: October 11, at Jacobs Field

The third game of the ALCS ended up being a pitching contest for the ages between Orel Hershiser and Baltimore's Mike Mussina. Hershiser held the Orioles to four hits and one walk over seven scoreless innings, while registering seven strikeouts. Mussina set a League Championship Series record, striking out fifteen batters. He allowed only three hits, but the Indians took the lead in the bottom of the seventh, as Mussina conceded an RBI-single to Matt Williams.

The game was all but won when José Mesa entered in the ninth inning. That was until Marquis Grissom, the hero of Game 1, lost track of Brady

---

[6] Grissom only had 12 home runs for the season, and only one of those (a grand slam against the Angels) had been for more than two RBI.

Anderson's fly ball, which dropped for a game-tying RBI double. The score remained tied, 1–1, into the bottom of the twelfth inning, when Grissom seized an opportunity to be the hero for the Tribe in a second consecutive game and make up for his costly mistake in the ninth.

Grissom drew a one-out walk and advanced to third base on a single to right field from Fernández. The Indians then had a squeeze play going with Omar Vizquel at the plate. Myers, the Orioles' closer, was a left-hander. With a man on base, he would be pitching from the stretch, meaning that his back would be turned to Grissom at third. As Myers started his delivery, Grissom darted for home. Vizquel squared around to bunt, and Myers' pitch, a breaking ball, found its way into the dirt around home plate, trickling past catcher Lenny Webster. Myers and Webster assumed Vizquel had fouled off the pitch. The shortstop walked to the right of home plate and turned around, so as to come back to the batter's box. Grissom continued his dash to home, crossing the plate standing up. Webster turned to hand the baseball to home plate umpire John Hirschbeck, who waved his arms to signal Grissom safe, and the Indians poured onto the field from the dugout to celebrate the victory. Davey Johnson raced from the visitors' dugout and waved his arms in protest, but Hirschbeck maintained his call, and Cleveland escaped Game 3 with a bizarre, 2–1 victory and the series lead.

Indians, 2; Orioles, 1

Game 4: October 12, at Jacobs Field

The momentum carried into Game 4. Cleveland overcame a one-run deficit in the second inning when Sandy Alomar Jr. hit a two-run homer to reclaim the lead. Baltimore jumped ahead in the third, scoring four runs off three home runs against starter Jaret Wright. The Tribe shortened the Orioles' lead to 5–3 in the fourth inning, and retook the lead on a strange play in the fifth. Scott Erickson had given up a home run to Ramírez and singles to Jim Thome, David Justice, and Sandy Alomar. With two outs, Johnson pulled Erickson and replaced him with Arthur Rhodes. Rhodes then walked Brian

Giles to load the bases. With Grissom at the plate, Rhodes uncorked a wild pitch. Webster, the catcher, couldn't get in front of Rhodes' misfire, and Justice hurried from third base to score. Webster made an errant toss to home in an attempt to cut down the runner at the plate, but Justice collided with Rhodes, who was covering, and the ball rolled freely toward the infield, allowing Alomar to score as well. The Indians took a 7–5 lead on the play.

Baltimore was able to score again in the seventh, pulling within a run of the Tribe, and Mesa gave up an RBI-single to Rafael Palmeiro, blowing another ninth-inning save opportunity. But with two outs in the bottom of the ninth, Sandy Alomar Jr. came to bat and single home Matt Williams for another walk-off victory. Cleveland now led the series, three games to one, with a chance to clinch the pennant the next day.

Indians, 8; Orioles, 7

Game 5: October 13, at Jacobs Field

Facing elimination, the Orioles were coming into Game 5 with a chance to send the series back to their home ballpark in Baltimore. They were facing Chad Ogea, whom they had already beaten once before in Game 1. The O's loaded the bases against Ogea in the third inning, and right fielder Gerónimo Berroa singled home two runs to establish the first lead. The score remained 2–0 after Scott Kamienicki and Jimmy Key stifled the Indians for eight innings. Baltimore added two more runs in the ninth inning off of Paul Assenmacher, including a homer by Eric Davis, to extend the lead to 4–0. Closer Randy Myers gave up RBI-doubles to Matt Williams and Tony Fernández, but ultimately thwarted the Indians' rally. The Orioles prevailed, 4–2, sending the series back to Baltimore.

Orioles, 4; Indians, 2

Game 6: October 15, at Oriole Park at Camden Yards

The Orioles faced elimination for a second time, but were at an advantage playing in front of their home fans. Game 6 featured another prime pitching matchup, this time pitting Mussina against Nagy. Mussina dazzled for eight scoreless innings of one-hit baseball, in which he fanned ten batters. Nagy threw 7.1 innings without giving up a run, before Hargrove went to his bullpen. The game remained scoreless into the eleventh inning, when the series took another twist.

During batting practice, Tony Fernández hit a ball that struck and bruised teammate Bip Roberts. Roberts had been fielding another ground ball when the line drive off the bat of Fernández drilled him in the back of his left hand. Roberts' hand, which had been surgically repaired once before, swelled in such a way that he had to be scratched from the lineup, and Fernández ultimately took his spot. Surely it was Fernández who came to the plate in the eleventh inning to face Armando Benítez with a chance to put the Indians ahead. Mussina watched from the dugout as Benítez hung a first-pitch slider up in the strike zone. Fernández smacked the pitch into the first row of seats above the light-up out-of-town scoreboard in right field, giving the Indians a 1–0 lead.

While the Indians had all the momentum, Baltimore had a chance to answer back in the bottom of the eleventh. José Mesa quickly retired Chris Hoiles and Lenny Webster for the first two outs of the inning, before giving up a single to Brady Anderson. With Anderson, the potential tying run, on base, Roberto Alomar stepped into the batter's box. Mesa and Alomar battled to a full count. Alomar recoiled on a 3–2 offering from Mesa to the inner part of the plate, taking the pitch. He was astonished when the home plate umpire called it strike three, ending the game and the series.

Roberto Alomar couldn't believe it was over, as his brother closed his mitt on the called third strike. Mussina certainly couldn't. He tallied 23 strikeouts in the series, breaking playoff records previously set by Bob Gibson, Tom Seaver, and Sandy Koufax. Eight of his punch-outs came against the eventual series MVP, Marquis Grissom. Never before had a team won four one-run games in the entire history of the League Championship Series. The Indians hit .193 as a team, but still managed to move ahead to the World Series for the second time in three years. The rest of the Orioles were in disbelief, but the Tribe believed more than ever that 1997 was finally going to be their year.

Indians, 1; Orioles, 0

Chapter Twenty-Eight

SEVEN IN '97

The 1997 World Series gave the Tribe an opportunity for redemption when they came back empty-handed against Atlanta in '95; for an early exit from the postseason in '96; for a city that longed for a winner. That opportunity came against the Florida Marlins.

Although the Marlins finished the regular season trailing the Braves by nine games in the National League East, the Miami-area expansion franchise's 92–70 record was good enough to capture its first playoff berth in club history as the Wild Card team.

These weren't your typical underdogs: General manager Dave Dombrowski got the go-ahead from owner Wayne Huizenga to sign high-priced free agents to bolster his roster. Payroll jumped from the bottom-half of the league ($25 million) in 1996 to the fifth highest ($52.5 million) in 1997. In two years leading up to their World Series appearance, the Marlins signed: third baseman Bobby Bonilla; left fielder Moisés Alou; center fielder Devon White; and starting pitchers Kevin Brown and Al Leiter. Those deals supplemented a squad that had: Jeff Conine, whom the Marlins picked in the expansion draft; catcher Charles Johnson, their first-round selection in the '92 amateur draft; Gary Sheffield, for whom Dombrowski traded in '93; Colombian shortstop Edgar Rentería, who previously signed as a sixteen-year-old and developed in their farm system; and right-hander Liván Hernández, who defected from Cuba and debuted as a twenty-one-year-old in September of '96. Over the course of the '97 season, Dombrowski also traded for Cliff Floyd and Darren Daulton.

Florida also had a proven manager in the dugout. The Marlins went through three different managers in 1996 before turning to Jim Leyland, who had twice been named NL Manager of the Year while at the helm for the Pittsburgh Pirates. Leyland was hired in 1997 and managed the Marlins to the World Series in only their fifth season, the shortest amount of time for any expansion club in MLB history until the Arizona Diamondbacks won the 2003 World Series after joining the league as an expansion team in 2001.

World Series

Game 1: October 18, at Pro Player Stadium

The National League had been assigned home-field advantage through the World Series, and Game 1 took place at Miami's Pro Player Stadium, which the Marlins shared with the NFL's Miami Dolphins. Sixty-seven thousand fans turned out to watch Hernández, the young Cuban, take on Indians veteran Orel Hershiser. The NLCS MVP, Hernández posted a 0.84 ERA, struck out 16 batters in 10.2 innings, and picked up two wins against Atlanta. He wasn't as sharp in his first World Series appearance, allowing the Indians to score first on a leadoff double by Bip Roberts and an RBI single by David Justice. But the Marlins countered, scoring seven runs off the elder Hershiser and knocking him out of the game in the fifth inning. Hernández and the Marlins took a 7–4 victory to open the Series on a high note.

Marlins, 7; Indians, 4

Game 2: October 19, at Pro Player Stadium

Whereas the Marlins had momentum, the Indians had experience. Cleveland had dropped the first game in each of the previous two series on their way to the Fall Classic. In each case, the Tribe engineered comebacks and were able to prevail. For Chad Ogea, their starter for Game 2, this was especially important. Ogea had gone 0–2 in the ALCS against the Orioles and was looking to improve in the World Series opposite Marlins ace Kevin Brown.

The game was tied at 1–1 after the first inning, benefiting from RBI singles by David Justice and Jeff Conine. The game stayed even until the fifth inning, when Cleveland mounted a rally, scoring three runs—thanks to singles by Matt Williams, Sandy Alomar Jr., Marquis Grissom, and Bip Roberts. They pushed Ogea's lead to five runs in the next frame, when Alomar hit a two-run homer off Brown. There the score remained, with the Indians taking the second game, 6–1, as the Series headed to Cleveland.

Indians, 6; Marlins, 1

Game 3: October 21, at Jacobs Field

The Indians and Marlins treated the Cleveland fans to a slugfest with a combined 26 hits in Game 3. Gary Sheffield's solo homer to left field in the top of the first opened the scoring, and lead changed hands four more times thereafter. The Tribe pulled ahead, 2–1, in the bottom of the first, on a pair of RBI singles by Matt Williams and Sandy Alomar Jr. Charles Nagy then gave up a single to Charles Johnson and a trio of walks in the top of the third, bringing the score level. Darren Daulton added a solo homer off Nagy in the fourth, helping the Marlins retake the lead, 3–2. That's when Florida starter Al Leiter encountered control problems of his own.

Leiter walked Alomar, Jim Thome, Marquis Grissom, and Omar Vizquel in the bottom of the fourth. Alomar scored on the walk by Vizquel, tying the game at three. Manny Ramírez then followed with a weak grounder to Bobby Bonilla at third base, and reached on a single, scoring Thome. Trying to get Ramírez at first, Bonilla made an errant throw, and Grissom came around to score from second base, making the score 5–3. Thome continued the onslaught by hitting a two-run homer to deep right field off Leiter in the bottom of the fifth, extending Cleveland's lead to 7–3.

The Marlins countered in the sixth, when Jim Eisenreich took Nagy deep for a two-run homer. After an RBI single and double from Rentería and Sheffield in the seventh, the Indians' lead had disappeared. Cleveland then fell apart defensively behind Eric Plunk in the ninth inning, allowing the Marlins to score seven runs on four hits and three errors. Although the Indians plated four runs off Marlins closer Rob Nen, they could not overcome the deficit at the end of Game 3 and lost, 14–11.

Marlins, 14; Indians, 11

Game 4: October 22, at Jacobs Field

Cleveland—not the Indians—made history the next night. The game-time temperature, 38°F, was the coldest in World Series history, with some of the wind chill readings being reported as low as 18°F. Days earlier, the Indians' players and their families had been relaxing poolside at the team hotel in Miami; in Cleveland, snow flurries fell during batting practice. The playing conditions favored the Indians, who started Jaret Wright opposite another rookie, Florida's Tony Saunders. The Tribe pulled ahead on a two-run homer from Manny Ramírez in the first inning. Matt Williams, who reached base six times in the contest, sealed a 10–3 victory with a two-run bomb in the bottom of the eighth.

Indians, 10; Marlins, 3

Game 5: October 23, at Jacobs Field

For a second time in the Series, Hernández competed against Hershiser. Unlike Game 1, the Marlins scored first in support of Hernández, with Charles Johnson and Devon White driving in two runs in the second inning. But Sandy Alomar Jr. continued his hot-streak in the postseason, delivering an RBI single to right field in the bottom of the second and a three-run homer in the third, giving the Indians a 4–2 lead.

The game turned in the sixth inning, when a three-run shot from Moisés Alou gave the Marlins back the lead, with the score now 5–4. Hargrove made two pitching changes later in the inning; the first was bringing in Alvin Morman, who walked Craig Counsell (the only batter he faced). Hargrove then brought in Plunk, who walked White to score Conine and extend Florida's lead by another run. Alou later padded the Marlins' lead with a ninth-inning single. Hernández gave way to Nen in the bottom of the ninth, with runners on the corners and the score 8–4.

The Tribe pulled to within one run on RBI singles from David Justice and Jim Thome. The crowd held its breath for a moment when Alomar hit a fly ball to deep right field, but Sheffield caught it for the third out. The Marlins won, 8–7, with Hernández picking up his second victory of the Series over Hershiser.

Marlins, 6; Indians, 7

Game 6: October 25, at Pro Player Stadium

The Marlins took the series lead back to warmer weather in Miami. Game 6 drew a crowd of 67,498 fans, the highest single-game attendance for a World Series game since 1959, when 92,706 saw Game 5 between the Dodgers and White Sox at Los Angeles Memorial Coliseum. This crowd came hoping to see the Marlins to a victory, which would clinch their first championship in franchise history. Chad Ogea wanted to see no part of it, and provided the Tribe with a strong outing. Ogea helped his cause in the top of the fifth inning, leading off with a double and scoring on a sacrifice fly from Manny Ramírez. Cleveland went on to win Game 6, 4–1, sending the World Series to a winner-take-all seventh game for the thirty-third time in MLB history.

Indians, 4; Marlins, 1

Game 7: October 26, at Pro Player Stadium

The final contest of the '97 series fell on Mike Hargrove's forty-eighth birthday. The last time the Indians played a World Series game on the skipper's birthday, Cleveland beat Atlanta, 5–4, avoiding elimination in Game 5 of the '95 World Series. With the Series again on the line, that should have been a good omen, right? The Indians manager had a critical decision to make. Would he start Jaret Wright, who earned a victory in Game 4, or would he go with Charles Nagy, the starter from Game 3. Starting Wright meant sending the rookie to the mound on short rest—in the World Series, no less. On the other hand, although Nagy was rested, he wasn't sharp in his last outing against the Marlins. Nagy allowed the solo home run to Gary Sheffield, another homer to Darren Daulton, and had problems finding the strike zone all night. By that logic, Hargrove went with the hot hand, and elected to start Wright. This looked like the right decision: Through the first six innings, Wright held the Marlins scoreless on one hit, and the Indians defended a 2–0 lead against Al Leiter.

Sure enough, the outcome started to turn in the seventh inning. Bobby Bonilla led off the inning with a solo home run to right-center on the first pitch to shorten the lead to one run. After Wright issued back-to-back walks, Hargrove brought in Paul Assenmacher to try and get the Indians out of the jam. The left-hander prevailed, preserving Cleveland's lead.

The Indians missed their chance to add an insurance run in the ninth, when Sandy Alomar Jr. was thrown out at home on a fielder's choice hit by Marquis Grissom. The Indians proceeded to the bottom of the ninth inning, confident that José Mesa would close out the victory as he had done so many times before—and give the Tribe their first World Series victory in forty-nine years. However, as any Cleveland fan will tell you, that is *not* what happened.

Mesa started the ninth by allowing a single to the leadoff hitter, Moisés Alou, before striking out Bonilla for the first out. Catcher Charles Johnson followed and hit a line drive single into right field, which advanced Alou to third. Now the Marlins had two men aboard—including the man representing the tying run standing only 90 feet from home plate with one out in the inning.

At some point during the ninth inning, MLB officials whisked John Hart and Dick Jacobs away from their seats at Pro Player Stadium and led them to the visitors' clubhouse. Hart was superstitious and reluctant to leave his seat. He and Jacobs entered the room and found that a layer of plastic tarp already covered the players' lockers. Bottles of champagne sat on ice in coolers, waiting for the players to uncork them. The Commissioner's Trophy rested on a table. Jacobs could have reached out and touched it, if he so chose; instead, he opted to wait for its official presentation. The name Chad Ogea, who had picked up two victories for these would-be champion Indians, was about to be inscribed on the trophy that was going to be awarded to the would-be series MVP. But out on the field, the wiry Craig Counsell lifted a line drive deep to right field. Manny Ramírez caught the ball ahead of the warning track, but Alou scored from third without a throw to the plate, tying the game. Mesa finished the inning without additional damage, but he registered a blown save and gave the Marlins new life. Hart and Jacobs remained in the clubhouse, watching the game on a television in Mike Hargrove's office.

Mesa pitched a scoreless tenth inning, and after the Indians failed to score, Hargrove replaced his closer with Nagy.

Bonilla led off the bottom of the eleventh with a single. Trying to move the runner over, Zaun popped up a bunt for the first out, and Bonilla returned safely to first base, avoiding a potential double play. Counsell, the ninth-inning hero, followed Zaun, producing a ground ball to the right side of the infield. On any other night, this would have resulted in a routine double play to end the inning. However, this time the ball went under the second baseman Fernández' glove and into the outfield, allowing Bonilla to advance all the way to third. Nagy issued an intentional walk to the next batter, Jim Eisenreich, giving the Indians a play at any base. Devon White then stepped up to the plate, 0-for-5 on the day. On the first pitch from Nagy, White hit a ground ball right to Fernández. This time, he gathered the ball quickly and threw it home, cutting down Bonilla at the plate for the second out. This brought Edgar Rentería to the plate. After taking a breaking ball for strike one, Rentería lined a pitch back up the middle toward the pitcher, and the ball glanced off Nagy's glove and into center field. Counsell scampered down the third baseline with his arms raised overhead. He jumped on the plate, clenching his fists as he stomped home the winning run of the World Series.

Clubhouse attendants wheeled the coolers of champagne down the hall to the home clubhouse, and placed the plastic tarp over the Marlins' lockers.

Out on the field, Fernández hung his head, looking briefly across the field as the Marlins began to celebrate, and headed in from his position. Hargrove stared blankly from the dugout before departing to the clubhouse. Indians players and coaches filed into the tunnel and retreated to the clubhouse as well. Dick Jacobs greeted each one, shaking their hands as they came through the door.

Only Omar Vizquel remained in the dugout. There he sat, despondent. The shortstop watched from the bench, envious of the victors. That was supposed to be him celebrating; his teammates shouting and high-fiving. They promised they would come through in the World Series. Instead, they became the first team in baseball history to have taken a lead into the ninth inning of the deciding game and lost. How could that be?

The shortstop's eyes were transfixed on the field. The trophy presentation, which traditionally took place in the clubhouse, instead took place on the field. Bud Selig, the acting commissioner, handed the trophy to the Marlins personnel. When the time came to announce the most valuable player, Selig didn't call out Ogea's name. Liván Hernández' name replaced Ogea's on the trophy. The twenty-two-year-old was far from perfect in the Series (Cleveland registered a .944 OPS rating against him), but he led Florida's staff with two victories. Hernández also made for an emotional story. Cuban authorities granted his mother permission to fly to Miami for Game 7. Two years had passed since the last time he had seen her.

While the fans inside Pro Player Stadium buzzed, the inside of the Indians' clubhouse was like a funeral parlor.

"It was quiet, probably the way it should have been," Charlie Manuel remembered. "Nobody said anything. We let it slip away. The '97 team was more prepared for what to expect and just didn't get it done."

Players sat at their lockers. Some cried, emotionally and physically drained by the experience. They emptied their lockers and left the ballpark to return to Cleveland. On the plane, Dick Jacobs turned to his son, Jeff, clasping his hands together, and said, "Next year's going to be a great year, too."

Marlins, 3; Indians, 2

Chapter Twenty-Nine

ONE-THOUSAND RUNS

Dick Jacobs was right. Next year was going to be a great year, too. The Indians welcomed back Kenny Lofton, who signed as a free agent in the offseason. The Tribe drew sellout crowds, plated runs in bunches, and marched on to win a fourth-consecutive title in the American League Central. This time, their championship hopes were dashed in the League Championship Series, as they lost to the New York Yankees in six games. John Hart retooled his ball club for the 1999 season, adding perennial All-Star second baseman Roberto Alomar. Roberto signed a four-year deal, which reunited him with his older brother, catcher Sandy Alomar Jr.

Roberto Alomar was a decorated infielder, having won eight straight Gold Glove Awards at second base for the Toronto Blue Jays and Baltimore Orioles. In joining the Indians, he would play opposite Omar Vizquel, a six-time winner, to create one of the most skilled double-play tandems in baseball history.

"It was like playing video games," Vizquel said. "I don't think I ever worked with another second baseman with the tools that Robbie had."

Coach Mike Hargrove agreed, stating, "I never got tired of coming to the ballpark and watching them play, fully expecting something that I had never seen before."

They were so skilled that the manager scheduled around their pregame routine to stop and watch.

"I used to purposely make sure I was doing nothing else during batting practice, when Omar and Robbie would work on double plays and their timing, not to see if they were doing it right. They would get their work in and then start showboating and fancy stuff. It's just absolutely amazing at what good defensive people can do with their gloves and their arms. I don't know that there has been a double-play combo like that, maybe [Lou] Whitaker and [Alan] Trammell, that had the athleticism and range that they did."[1]

Aside from being one of the premier defenders in baseball, Roberto was one of the top hitters, as well. He had hit above .300 in six of the previous seven seasons and was twice named a Silver Slugger before coming to Cleveland. His acquisition upgraded Hargrove's lineup heading into '99:

Opening Day Lineup:

CF	*Kenny Lofton*
SS	*Omar Vizquel*
2B	*Roberto Alomar*
1B	*Jim Thome*
RF	*Manny Ramírez*
LF	*David Justice*
3B	*Travis Fryman*
DH	*Wil Cordero*

---

[1] Second baseman Lou Whitaker and shortstop Alan Trammell formed the longest-running double-play combination in major-league history, playing together from the time of their debuts in 1977 through the 1995 season. They combined for seven Gold Glove awards between them.

C   *Sandy Alomar Jr.*

Lofton, the leadoff man, hit for a .301 average (his sixth .300 season in seven years), and got on base at a .405 clip. The switch-hitting Vizquel followed, recording a career-high .333 average to out-hit even his double-play partner. Roberto Alomar did damage in the third spot of the lineup: He hit .323, tallied 24 homers, 120 runs batted in, and swiped 37 bases. Thome, the cleanup hitter, smacked 33 home runs. But nobody on the '99 club could match the performance of Manny Ramírez. Hitting in the fifth spot, the right fielder recorded a .333 average, launched 44 home runs, and drove in an Indians franchise record 165 runs. His RBI total was the highest since Jimmie Foxx amassed 175 for the Boston Red Sox in 1938.[2]

Justice and Cordero gave the lineup steady production in the bottom half of the order, with Fryman and Alomar Jr. missing significant portions of the season due to injury. A platoon of Enrique Wilson, Carlos Baerga, and others filled in for Fryman, while Einar Díaz caught 108 games in place of Alomar.

By the conclusion of the regular season, the Indians had managed to score more than 1,000 runs, averaging a league-high 6.1 runs per game. This was a significant accomplishment. Since 1901, only six major-league teams had topped the 1,000-run mark in a season. The feat had taken place five times in the 1930s (three of them by teams with Babe Ruth), and prior to the Indians, the last club to do it was the Boston Red Sox in 1950. Suddenly, the Indians were being viewed among some of the elite offensive clubs in the history of the game. That is because, from 1994 into the 2001 season, they were.

One method of assessing an individual player's career performance is to analyze his statistics over a span of seven years, generally starting around the season the player turns twenty-seven years old. This stretch of seasons is traditionally referenced in the sabermetric community as his seven-year peak, or what the average fan at the ballpark would call the player's prime. Some players are able to establish themselves outside of this range, with Manny

---

[2] Since Ramírez' 165 RBI season, the only player to come close to that number was Sammy Sosa, who had 160 RBI in 2001; a season in which he hit 64 home runs.

Ramírez being an example of one such player. Great teams will have a handful of players of a high caliber, whose prime years overlap. The Cleveland Indians were fortunate that the core of their lineup featured All-Star players whose prime years overlapped:

Kenny Lofton scored 829 runs for the Indians in that span. Apply the 90 runs he scored in one season in Atlanta, and he could have crossed home more times than any man in the American League, ahead of former Yankees Chuck Knoblauch and Bernie Williams. Otherwise, Lofton scored the fourth-most in the majors after Jeff Bagwell, Barry Bonds, and Craig Biggio. He also led baseball with 341 stolen bases, which doesn't look quite as impressive next to Rickey Henderson's 668 steals from 1980 to 1987, but make the case for Lofton as the prototypical leadoff man of the nineties.[3]

Along with Craig Biggio, Ryne Sandberg, and Bret Boone, **Carlos Baerga** and **Roberto Alomar** helped to usher in a wave of second basemen who could hit for both power and average. Jeff Kent, whom the Indians traded, hit more homers (194) than any other second baseman in the nineties, but Baerga and Alomar combined for 278.

Famed statistician Bill James once wrote that if Hall of Fame left fielder Willie Stargell had played in the nineties (his career spanned from 1962–82), his numbers would have looked a lot like **Albert Belle's**. In the first three years of the Jacobs Field-era, Belle, the cleanup hitter, compiled 134 home runs. His total surpassed Frank Thomas (118), Barry Bonds (112), Mo Vaughn (109), and Andrés Galarraga (109) for the most in baseball, before departing for the White Sox. He also had the active lead in consecutive games played when Cal Ripken Jr. ended his streak.[4]

---

[3] And also take into account that Rickey Henderson was the greatest leadoff man in baseball history, as well as having 468 more stolen bases than anyone else in the sport, all-time.

[4] Ripken ended his streak at 2,632 consecutive games played. Belle became the active leader for consecutive games, at 327.

Jim Thome and **Manny Ramírez** averaged 32 and 33 home runs per year,[5] respectively, from 1994 to 2000. Each player was just entering his seven-year peak toward the end of that stretch. Thome hit 101 homers over the next two seasons, establishing a new Indians franchise record with 334 home runs before departing for the Philadelphia Phillies as a free agent. Ramírez' career surged thereafter, as well, but after he signed with the Boston Red Sox.

Even more astounding is how the Indians fared, historically, among baseball's classic clubs. We are able to do this by virtue of advanced metrics. Bill James sought to answer how many runs a player was worth to his team in a given season. His solution was a statistic called Runs Created (RC), which attempted to quantify a player's offensive value. Tom Tango, another analyst, refined the James statistic, devising Weighted Runs Created (wRC). Tango's statistic was based off of a player's weighted on-base average (wOBA, a popular stat), which applies scaling factors to all the outcomes that could possibly result from plate appearances (walks, singles, doubles, etc.) in proportion to their actual run values. (Is a single worth as much as a double? And so forth.) Weighted Runs Created Plus (wRC+) takes the Tango statistic and normalizes it against the league average. The system for wRC+ establishes the league average at 100, so that every point above or below 100 corresponds with one percentage point in relation to league average. For example, when the Indians registered a team wRC+ of 115 in 1995, it meant they scored runs at a rate that was 15 percentage points higher than the league average. (The next highest team was Boston at 107, which scored at a rate 7 percentage points above league average.) The value in wRC+ is that it creates a neutral run environment, allowing comparison between players and teams from the past and present. The booming years in the era of Babe Ruth differed from those of high mounds and low scoring in the time of Sandy Koufax, all the way through today. Weighted Runs Created Plus is park- and league-adjusted, giving the baseball community a method for comparing the all-time greats. These statistics are commonly used to determine a player's offensive value, and play a role in front-office trade and free-agent negotiations.

---

[5] The exact home-run figures are 31.8 (Thome) and 33.4 (Ramírez).

In their seven-year peak from 1994 through 2000, the Indians wRC+ (111) was 11 percentage points above league average. Their sustained run production over that span surpassed:

- **Mickey Mantle's Yankees** (109) from 1951 to 1957. Mantle is tied with Jim Thome for career walk-off home runs (13). He won three MVP awards in 1956, '57, and '62. During the latter stretch, the Yankees also welcomed Roger Maris, who broke Ruth's single-season home-run record (61 homers in 1961).
- **The Yankees** (109) from 1996 to 2002, when they won four championships with Derek Jeter, Jorge Posada, Bernie Williams, and others.
- **Joe DiMaggio's Yankees** (108) from 1936 to 1942, and again in the post-war years (106 from 1945–51).
- **The Cincinnati Reds' Big Red Machine** (107) from 1970 to 1976. The Reds were winners of four pennants and two World Series championships. Sparky Anderson's clubs averaged 98 wins per season. They had six league MVPs, four home-run champions, three batting champions, three future Hall-of-Famers (Johnny Bench, Tony Pérez, and Joe Morgan) and the all-time leader in hits, Pete Rose.
- **The Milwaukee Braves** (105) from 1955 to 1961. In a larger stretch of years (1953–63), Eddie Mathews and Hank Aaron combined for 850 of the 1,226 home runs they would hit as Braves, helping Milwaukee to two pennants and one World Series title.
- **The Brooklyn Dodgers** (104) from 1947 to 1953. Famously assembled by Branch Rickey, this was a team that featured Pee Wee Reese, Jackie Robinson, Gil Hodges, Duke Snider, and Roy Campanella. The Dodgers captured four NL pennants in 1947, '49, '52, and '53, losing to the Yankees each time.
- **The Seattle Mariners** clubs with Ken Griffey Jr., Jay Buhner, Edgar Martínez, and Alex Rodriguez would come to match the Indians' output, achieving a wRC+ of 111 from 1996 to 2002.

As one might expect, some teams have produced higher single-season totals. The 1982 Brewers recorded an eye-popping wRC+ of 120, the second-highest figure after the '76 Reds for a team without Babe Ruth on its roster. The champion '84 Tigers, another Sparky Anderson team, matched the '95 Tribe's 115, as did the 2013 Boston Red Sox.

Notably, two teams surpassed Cleveland's seven-year rate of offensive production. The more recent club to do so was the Yankees from 2003 to 2009. New York's offense performed at a rate that was 14 percent above league average. The lineup had as many as seven hitters with twenty or more home runs. But that doesn't even come close to the sustained offensive output of Babe Ruth and the Yankees of Murderers' Row. The Babe's teams remain the gold standard in single-season and sustained offensive production. In 1927, the New York Yankees' lineup performed at a rate 26 percent above the league average. The Bronx Bombers continued to score runs at a rate 20 percent above the rest of the league from 1926 to 1932. Ruth was the AL home-run champ each year, and he won three of four World Series titles with the Yankees during that span.

What's the takeaway from all this? Apart from the pennants and division crowns, the nineties Indians are winners of one other title: The offense performed at a higher rate over seven years than any other club that didn't win the World Series.

Chapter Thirty

THE SALE

It is important to remember that Dick Jacobs first approached the purchase of the Cleveland Indians franchise as a business venture. The owner didn't allow sentimentality to get in the way of that fact as he went about his dealings. With the Tribe's successes on and off the field during the nineties, Jacobs saw the Indians enter the upper echelon of lucrative sporting franchises. He was reminded of this in March of 1998, when Major League Baseball's owners approved the sale of the Los Angeles Dodgers to media mogul Rupert Murdoch's Fox group. Peter O'Malley, whose family owned the ball club since 1950 and moved it from Brooklyn, decided to sell the franchise. His deal included Dodger Stadium and 300 acres surrounding the ballpark in downtown Los Angeles; the team's spring training home in Vero Beach, Florida; and Campo Las Palmas, the Dodgers' baseball academy in Santo Domingo, Dominican Republic. The package carried a $311 million price tag.

Always looking for additional opportunities for business, Jacobs looked to the market for a way to make money on his investment while maintaining control of the franchise. The solution, he decided, was to make the Indians the first publicly traded MLB franchise. Other pro sports teams were being

215

traded on Wall Street, including the NBA's Boston Celtics, the NFL's Green Bay Packers, and the nascent Florida Panthers of the NHL. The Indians' initial public offering was priced at $15 per share and hit the market in June of 1998 as CLEV. Jacobs released four million common shares, and had an additional 600,000 waiting if the stock had high enough demand. The public offering raised another $60 million in revenue. Jacobs watched the price creep up during the 1999 season as the Tribe's offense boomed.

However, the Indians suffered a monumental collapse against the Boston Red Sox in the American League Division Series. The Red Sox scored forty-four runs over the final three games of the series, including a postseason-record twenty-three in Game 4. Boston's offensive onslaught prompted Cleveland's disappointing first-round elimination from the playoffs. Four days after their defeat, John Hart decided the Indians needed a new leader. Hart said in a news conference that he needed a manager who could take his club to the next level, and made the difficult choice to relieve Mike Hargrove of his duties. After taking over a team that lost 105 games in 1991, Hargrove finished just seven wins shy of Lou Boudreau's franchise-record 728 victories.[1]

Jacobs had been mulling the decision to sell the Indians, and in November of '99, he finally agreed to a deal with another Cleveland-area native, Larry Dolan.

Dolan had previously made a bid of $525 million to buy the expansion Browns' NFL franchise, but in 1998, the league voted in favor of Al Lerner, a friend of former Browns owner Art Modell, who bought the team for a record $476 million. This motivated Dolan to pursue the Indians.

"There's a time to hold and a time to fold," Jacobs said at a news conference with Dolan in November of '99. That time was fast approaching. Within the next three years, the Indians would have to consider forking over hundreds of millions of dollars to young stars like Manny Ramírez and Jim

---

[1] Hargrove also bested Boudreau in winning percentage (.564 to .528) and average wins per season (86.1 to 80.8). These stats only count full seasons, as Hargrove was hired mid-1991, managing the final 85 games of the season.

Thome, whose contracts were expiring. Jacobs rejected Dolan's initial bid of $275 million, but the two agreed on a deal as the regular season approached early the following year. The sale became official in February of 2000, as Dolan paid $323 million for the franchise Jacobs and his brother bought for $35 million in 1986, to which Jacobs told the media, "I don't think I'll suffer from seller's remorse."

The sale, which did not include Jacobs Field, set a new baseball record, surpassing the Dodgers' mark in 1998. Dolan also bought all the team's stock off the market at about $22.50 a share to take sole ownership of the franchise.

Dolan retained John Hart as his general manager, and Hart tapped hitting coach Charlie Manuel as Mike Hargrove's replacement in the dugout. Despite winning 90 games in his first season, Manuel's club narrowly missed the playoffs.[2] The Chicago White Sox, winners of 95 games, captured their first AL Central title.[3] Then, as Jacobs suspected, the free agents began to depart. Ramírez left town that offseason, taking the Red Sox' offer of eight years, $160 million. Despite the pleas from his teammates, coaches and the front office, Ramírez turned down a similar deal from the Indians worth $160 million. (His agent at the time, Jeff Moorad, told media that more of the money in the Indians' offer was deferred.) Sandy Alomar Jr. signed a two-year, $5.4 million deal with the White Sox on December 18, 2000.

Hart announced before the 2001 season that it would be his last as the Indians' general manager. Fittingly, the Tribe claimed the AL Central. However, they lost the ALDS in five games to the Seattle Mariners, a club that tied the 1908 Chicago Cubs' major-league record of 116 regular-season victories. On December 11, Roberto Alomar was traded away with minor leaguers Danny Peoples and Mike Bacsik to the New York Mets for players to be named later (Alex Escobar, Matt Lawton, and Jerrod Riggan, and later

---

[2] The Seattle Mariners were the AL Wild Card winners with a 91–71 record, half a game better than the Indians.

[3] The AL Central was formed in 1994, and the Sox were in first place until the strike ended the season.

Earl Snyder and Billy Traber), signaling a dreaded era of rebuilding upcoming for Hart's replacement, Mark Shapiro. The next winter, Jim Thome signed a six-year, $85 million contract to join the Philadelphia Phillies. Kenny Lofton signed with the Pittsburgh Pirates. The last of the core Indians to leave was Omar Vizquel, who signed with the San Francisco Giants in November of 2004. The golden era was officially over.

* * *

On June 5, 2009, Dick Jacobs passed away at the age of eighty-three. The lasting impact of his Tribe's revival continued to be seen around baseball on the field and in the front office. On the field, six former Indians players from the late eighties and early nineties became big-league managers, including Charlie Manuel (Cleveland and Philadelphia); Terry Francona (Philadelphia, Boston, and Cleveland); John Farrell (Toronto and Boston); Ron Washington (Texas); Bud Black (San Diego); and Sandy Alomar Jr. (Cleveland, interim basis). Charles Nagy served as the pitching coach for the Arizona Diamondbacks and Los Angeles Angels. Dennis Martínez spent one season as the Houston Astros' bullpen coach. Wayne Kirby coached in the Indians and Rangers organizations before becoming the first base coach for the Baltimore Orioles. The Los Angeles Angels hired Omar Vizquel as an infield coach in 2013; he joined the Detroit Tigers in 2014 as their first base coach, and manages today in the White Sox organization. Jim Thome joined the White Sox in July of 2013 as a special assistant to the club's senior vice president and general manager, Rick Hahn.

The leadership ring that formed out of Hank Peters and Tom Giordano's influence in the front office extended past John Hart to his assistants. What resulted could be compared to the NFL coaching trees that stemmed from Mike Holmgren and the late Bill Walsh.

"As kind of the older baseball sage, I remember we used to talk a lot sitting in my office, and we had these young, bright guys," Hart said. "The only missing piece in their resume was the ability to connect the dots with the players. One of the things I'm most proud about is not only the ability to have had a great team, but to develop in that era a great front-office staff with a philosophy and a vision that was spread a lot through baseball. Guys out there really cut their teeth in our front office, and I pull for every one of them. Hank set the mark. They had a great front-office group in Baltimore with John Schuerholz, Harry Dalton, Frank Cashen, a tremendous group that came together in the sixties and seventies era in Baltimore that all came from Paul Richards."

Hart's disciples ascended from their roles as assistants to become top executives in front offices around Major League Baseball. They included Mark Shapiro and Chris Antonetti in Cleveland; Dan O'Dowd in Colorado; Paul DePodesta in Los Angeles; Neal Huntington in Pittsburgh; Ben Cherington and Mike Hazen in Boston, and later in Arizona; Josh Byrnes in Arizona; and Jon Daniels in Texas.

EPILOGUE

Back in 1995, during a film session with Major League Baseball Productions, Omar Vizquel looked into the camera and made a prophetic comment. "This has been one of the most exciting seasons for any team in baseball. I think it's going to be hard just to tell somebody in 2010 the kind of lineup we had in 1995. These guys are able to do really weird stuff, just coming back from behind, winning the game in the last at-bat. It has just been an unbelievable season and . . . nobody can forget what kind of team we had in this 1995 season."

If only Vizquel knew then how he and his teammates would perform in the seasons that followed. The Tribe's high-powered offense helped Cleveland to six division titles and two American League pennants over seven years.

"We had the team to win a couple," said former hitting coach and manager Charlie Manuel. "We could've, should've won a couple. Atlanta won fourteen of fifteen division championships. The one [World Series] they won got them off the hook. For some reason, that didn't happen for us while we were there."

"Every time we stepped between the lines, we went in there to kill people!" said second baseman Carlos Baerga. "I was talking to Derek Jeter and Bernie Williams, those guys came to me saying, 'Carlos, I want to tell you something. Everybody's always talking about the Yankees. But every time the Cleveland Indians come to New York, or we go to Cleveland. . . . We hate you guys, because you are so cocky. The confidence you guys have is unbelievable, and we know we're going to get killed.' There's Derek Jeter, a future Hall of Famer talking like that. That means the lineup we had was unbelievable."

It really is fitting that the city and its baseball franchise experienced a period of renaissance together in 1995. That was owner Dick Jacobs' true vision. Cleveland unveiled the Rock and Roll Hall of Fame and Museum. World-recognized architect I. M. Pei designed the museum's exterior so that it would resemble a turntable on a massive record player. The glass pyramid at the entrance of the Rock Hall, as locals call it, would make the building one of Cleveland's unmistakable landmarks on the Lake Erie waterfront north of the downtown area. Rock royalty showed up to commemorate the museum's official opening in September of 1995, with a benefit concert next door at Municipal Stadium, featuring an All-Star lineup including Chuck Berry, Bob Dylan, Jerry Lee Lewis, Johnny Cash, John Fogerty, and Bruce Springsteen, among others. One week later, the Indians clinched their first playoff appearance in forty-one years.

John Hart shared a similar sentiment.

"That really was *the* story in baseball. Here was a city that was down and out, a franchise that was down and out, and the two mirrored each other. I think the rise of the Indians and the rise of Cleveland sent a real good message."

For every home game of the baseball season from 1995 until 2001, fans packed Jacobs Field to see the Indians' rock show.

"The Indians didn't sell out games, they sold out seasons," *Plain Dealer* beat writer Paul Hoynes said.

They were the first club to sell out all eighty-one regular-season home games before Opening Day, when they did so in 1996.

"It's amazing to us that in Cleveland, Ohio, the Indians were the first to do that," said Bob DiBiasio, Indians vice president of public relations. "We did that five years in a row here."

The Tribe's streak of sellouts began June 12, 1995. Cleveland beat the Orioles that day, 4–3. From that day forward, the Indians managed to sell out 455 consecutive regular-season contests, a streak that ran until April 4, 2001. Not included in the streak are twenty-four playoff games and the 1997 All-Star Game, which were also sold out. It was the longest-running streak in major-league history until 2008, when the Boston Red Sox eventually surpassed it. The Sox' streak continued to 794 games before it ended in 2013.

Several factors contributed to the Indians streak, including the novelty of the new ballpark, the renaissance in the downtown area, an era of economic growth in Cleveland, and the departure of the Cleveland Browns to Baltimore in the winter of '95.

Hart contended that the Tribe's return to prominence, given the other conditions, was the only factor to ensure the streak continued.

"We made great decisions on players, we didn't miss on them. That's a part of the baseball evaluation process. We knew our players and we were able to make good calls on them. We were sort of a beacon for a lot of the markets that wanted to get new stadiums," he recalled.

"I spent a lot of time talking to media from those markets, who were like, 'Oh, a new stadium, and look what happened in Cleveland.' I would tell them, 'I'm going to tell you something: A new stadium will help, but at the end of the day, the game is about the players. Just because you're going to have financially more to dip into, you're not going to be able to change the fact that you're going to have to have good players to make this work.'"

Former manager Mike Hargrove said, "It happened here first, which I think shocked the hell out of a lot of people around the country. For the longest time, Cleveland has always gotten a bad rep and the brunt of bad jokes. I think the fact that our fans responded so well and so excitedly to our ball club made it a real special time."

The Indians commemorated the streak, retiring No. 455 to honor "The Fans," alongside Bob Feller, Larry Doby, Bob Lemon, Mel Harder, Earl Averill, Lou Boudreau, and Jackie Robinson.

"I don't know that fans understand how they can affect a team's performance. Not affect it to the point that you're going to win or lose because of it, but how you could come out here sometimes after playing fifteen days in a row, guys are dragging and need a day off, it's hot, it's humid. Contrary to what people might believe, players don't get to the ballpark at 6:30 to play the game at 7. They're here at one o'clock and don't get to go home before one in the morning a lot of times. To step out onto the field and be dragging a little bit, and to hear the buzz that was in the ballpark from the people, the applause and the cheers was really uplifting for all of us. There were many a night where we'd get into big situations and our fans would start that rumble, and it was like this energy, this ball of energy coming at you, and our players accepted that and did something special. They threw that ball of energy right back and forth. So I really came to understand the importance of having energetic and loyal fans."

That's also because the Indians have had fans like John Adams.

Born in 1951, Adams started attending games with his father at Municipal Stadium. Adams bought a 26-inch bass drum for $25 from a listing in the *Trade-n-Times* paper in Cleveland, and decided to lug it to the ballpark for a game in August. Adams, twenty-one, sat in the bleachers and beat his drum, hoping to rally the Indians. The Tribe beat the Rangers, 11–5. A reporter from the *Cleveland Press* wrote in an article that Adams would again be playing his drum at the ballpark the next day, despite Adams having told him that he wouldn't. When he saw it in print, he decided to return to Municipal Stadium, bass drum in tow.

More than forty years later, Adams said he's missed only thirty-eight games. The late Indians broadcaster Herb Score nicknamed Adams "Big Chief Boom-Boom." Today he sits in the top row of the left-field bleachers at Progressive Field, and has a regimented pattern. Adams beats the drum once the Indians take the field. He'll strike it whenever they have runners in scoring position, or in the late innings with the team tied or losing. His favorite time to hit it is before the last out of a victory in the top of the ninth inning. He normally starts with a slow beat, which gets progressively faster with each pitch. His rules are that he must bring the beat to a halt when the pitcher comes set, and that the game dictates his pace.

"He's like a part of the team. He's a tradition. He's been there so many years that sometimes we don't even notice it any more—you expect it," former Indians catcher, manager, and current first base coach Sandy Alomar Jr. said. "I think you notice it more if you don't hear the beat. It's like, 'Oh, wait a minute, this guy's not here.' He's out there every single game, if it's cold, sunny or rainy. He's a true fan."

The drumming has turned Adams into somewhat of a cult celebrity around town. The team honored Adams with a commemorative bobble-head after his 3,000th game in 2011. People come to the box-office ticket window specifically asking to sit next to him. One fan traveled from as far as Japan, specifically requesting to sit beside the drummer. Adams insists he's just a typical Clevelander who works a regular day job, but still hauls his drum to ball games. "It weights two ounces when we win, and it weighs 200 pounds when we lose," he said.

There was a stretch following the sellout streak when the drum must have felt like it weighed 200 pounds more nights than not. The Indians finished with losing records eight times from 2002–2012. Not to be overlooked is the 2007 season, when the club posted 96 wins but fell to the eventual champion Red Sox in seven games in the ALCS.

More recently, the Tribe has enjoyed another resurgence under President of Baseball Operations Chris Antonetti's direction. He hired skipper Terry Francona before the 2013 season and re-orchestrated the club's roster. As a result, the Indians won 92 games and returned to the playoffs as one of the two AL Wild Card teams, with Francona winning the AL Manager of the Year Award. With Tito at the helm, the Tribe have won three straight division titles

(2016–2018), punctuated by the 2016 AL crown. The excitement around the Tribe drew so much attention that Major League Baseball awarded the club the 2019 All-Star Game.

In the meantime, Tribe fans still wait for that elusive World Series title, which would be the club's first since 1948.

Said Hall-of-Fame slugger Jim Thome: "These fans deserve it. They've waited so long."

ACKNOWLEDGMENTS

I've heard that part of finding success is being in the right place at the right time. The right places for me have been Cleveland in the mid-'90s, and the Tampa Bay area in the late-2000s. I wanted to write this book and contribute a portion of the proceeds to the Indians Charities so the Tribe may continue to inspire young fans like it did for me. I want to thank God for blessing me with this opportunity and the resources to see it through.

I'd like to extend a special thanks to my family and friends for their support throughout the duration of this project. Mom, Baba, Michael, Alex: You have allowed me to monopolize dinner conversations at home with talk about the book for almost four years with little to no protest. I promise all of you that we can finally talk about something else now.

I had not yet met my wife, Morgan, when this book first went to press in 2014, but it's fitting that so many years after my family moved from Cleveland to Florida, I wound up marrying a girl from Chagrin Falls, Ohio. I'm so glad you, Dad, Doug, Nanny, and the rest of the Libers share an appreciation for the Tribe and the book!

Baba, Papou George, Uncle Bill, and Cousin Christopher: Thank you for taking me to my first game back in July of 1994. When I think of baseball in its purest form, the image in my mind is the view from the left-field bleacher seats adjacent to Albert's "Home Run Porch." A special thanks to Chris for being a sounding board throughout the entire writing process.

T-Bone, I owe you an unlimited supply of my mom's avgolemono (Greek chicken soup) after all of your help. You recruited the majority of people who granted interviews for the book, and have been my closest friend and mentor around Major League Baseball.

Hank Peters, thank you for sharing your insights in our interviews and the foreword. Many people told me that you were an ideal baseball man to emulate as I pursue my career, and now I know why.

John Hart, I won't forget our first phone conversation, when you pulled over to the side of the road in the mountains to address my questions for the book. I still can't believe we covered as much as we did. I'm glad I was able to be there to celebrate your induction into the Indians' Distinguished Hall of Fame with T-Bone and your lovely family.

I'd like to thank the following members (past and present) of the Indians organization for their contributions to the book: Bob DiBiasio, Senior Vice President of Public Affairs; and Bart Swain, Director of Baseball Information; scouts Mickey White, Tom Couston, and Joe DeLucca; former managers Mike Hargrove, Charlie Manuel, John McNamara, and coaches Mark Wiley and Rick Wolff; players Sandy Alomar Jr., Carlos Baerga, Dennis Martínez, Jim Thome and Omar Vizquel; team internist Dr. Bill Wilder; and announcer Tom Hamilton.

Dr. Jim and the Honorable Ellie Threlkel: Thanks for welcoming the Indians and their fans to Winter Haven, Florida, and for taking the time to share your memories with me.

John Adams, the Indians have marched to the beat of your drum for more than forty years. There are super fans, and then there is John Adams. This book wouldn't be complete without your memories from the bleachers.

ACKNOWLEDGMENTS

Jeffrey P. Jacobs, your father helped save baseball for me and for all of Cleveland, for which I am very grateful. I would have loved to have spoken with him. Thank you for giving me a vantage point into the life of Dick Jacobs.

Jason Katzman, it's been a pleasure putting this book together with you. You've been the best (and only) book editor I've ever had.

Ken Samelson, I couldn't have landed this publishing deal without your persistence.

Mike Foley, you sponsored a few independent study projects while I was at the University of Florida so I could write this book, and gave me an A grade without ever really seeing much of it. I hope the final product is worth the grade.

Eli Marger, there's nobody else I know who would appreciate random text messages containing some of the more obscure baseball names I came across in the process of writing this book. I'm glad I could always pick up the phone and talk sabermetrics with you.

To everyone else who played a part in making this book a reality, I'm grateful for your efforts.

—George Pappas

SOURCES

Twenty years have passed since the Indians moved into Progressive (formerly Jacobs) Field. I was only two years old when the ballpark opened its gates for the first time. I am grateful for several players, coaches, team personnel, and media for relating their experiences and memories.

Personal Interviews

John Adams: Cleveland Indians #1 fan, drummer at more than 3,000 games since 1973.

Sandy Alomar Jr.: First base coach, Cleveland Indians; catcher, San Diego Padres, Indians, Chicago White Sox, Colorado Rockies, Texas Rangers, Los Angeles Dodgers, New York Mets; 1990 AL Rookie of the Year, six-time All-Star, 1997 MLB All-Star Game MVP.

Carlos Baerga: Second baseman, Cleveland Indians, New York Mets, Boston Red Sox, Arizona Diamondbacks, Washington Nationals; three-time All-Star, two-time Silver Slugger.

Tom Couston: Thirty-eight years as area scouting supervisor, Tampa Bay Rays, Cleveland Indians, Arizona Diamondbacks.

Joe DeLucca: Retired scout, Cleveland Indians.

Bob DiBiasio: Senior Vice president, Public Affairs, Cleveland Indians.

Tom Giordano: Senior Advisor to Professional Scouting, Atlanta Braves; second baseman, Philadelphia Athletics; minor-league manager, Milwaukee Braves, Kansas City A's, Seattle Pilots; scout, Kansas City/Oakland Athletics, Pilots, Milwaukee Brewers, Montreal Expos, Indians; scouting director, Baltimore Orioles; farm director, Orioles; assistant to the president, Indians; Senior Advisor to the General Manager, Texas Rangers; 2007 East Coast Scout of the Year.

Tom Hamilton: Cleveland Indians radio announcer.

Mike Hargrove: Former manager, Cleveland Indians, Baltimore Orioles, Seattle Mariners; first baseman, Texas Rangers, San Diego Padres, Indians; 1974 AL Rookie of the Year, '75 AL All-Star.

John Hart: Studio analyst, MLB Network; Atlanta Braves President of Baseball Operations (2014-17) Baseball Operations, Atlanta Braves, Texas Rangers General Manager (2001-05), Senior Advisor (2005-13); minor-league catcher, Montreal Expos; minor-league manager, Baltimore Orioles; third-base coach, Orioles; special assignment scout, Cleveland Indians; manager, Indians; director of baseball operations, Indians; general manager, Indians, Rangers; *Sporting News* Major League Executive of the Year '94–95.

Paul Hoynes: Indians beat writer, *Cleveland Plain Dealer*.

Jeffrey P. Jacobs: Chairman and CEO, Jacobs Entertainment; Ohio House of Representatives ('82–86); son of former Indians owner Richard E. "Dick" Jacobs.

Charlie Manuel: Former manager, Cleveland Indians, Philadelphia Phillies; hitting coach, Indians; outfielder, Minnesota Twins, Los Angeles Dodgers, Yakult Swallows, Kintetsu Buffaloes; 2008 World Series Champion.

Dennis Martínez: Pitcher, Baltimore Orioles, Montreal Expos, Cleveland Indians, Seattle Mariners, Atlanta Braves; four-time All-Star, 1983

World Series Champion, pitched a perfect game July 28, 1991; former bullpen coach, Houston Astros; minor-league pitching coach, St. Louis Cardinals.

John McNamara: Former manager, Oakland A's, San Diego Padres, Cincinnati Reds, California Angels, Boston Red Sox, Cleveland Indians; 1986 AL Manager of the Year.

Hank Peters: Former general manager, Kansas City A's, Baltimore Orioles, Cleveland Indians; farm director, A's, Indians; assistant general manager, Indians; former president, National Association; *Sporting News* Executive of the Year 1979 and 1983.

Jim Thome: Special assistant to the general manager, Chicago White Sox; third/first baseman and designated hitter, Cleveland Indians, Philadelphia Phillies, White Sox, Los Angeles Dodgers, Minnesota Twins, Baltimore Orioles; five-time All-Star, 1996 Silver Slugger, 2002 Roberto Clemente Award, 2003 NL Home Run Champion, 612 career home runs; 2018 Hall of Fame inductee.

Dr. Jim and Honorable Ellie Threlkel: Former mayor, Winter Haven, Florida.

Omar Vizquel: First-base coach, Detroit Tigers; shortstop, Seattle Mariners, Cleveland Indians, San Francisco Giants, Texas Rangers, Chicago White Sox, Toronto Blue Jays; former infield coach, Los Angeles Angels of Anaheim; three-time All-Star, eleven-time Gold Glove Award winner; infield coach, Los Angeles Angels of Anaheim (2013); first base coach, Detroit Tigers (2014–17); minor league manager, Chicago White Sox (2018).

Mickey White: Professional scout; former scouting director, Cleveland Indians, Pittsburgh Pirates; former scout, Indians, Cincinnati Reds, Texas Rangers, Pittsburgh Pirates, Baltimore Orioles, Miami Marlins.

Dr. Bill Wilder: Former medical director, Cleveland Indians.

Mark Wiley: Director of pitching operations, Colorado Rockies; former pitching coach, Baltimore Orioles, Cleveland Indians, Kansas City Royals, Florida Marlins; pitcher, Minnesota Twins, San Diego Padres, Toronto Blue Jays.

Rick Wolff: Senior Executive Editor, Houghton Mifflin Harcourt; roving sports psychology coach, Cleveland Indians; minor-league second baseman, Detroit Tigers; Nationally-recognized in psychology of sports parenting.

Books

Cox, Ronald and Skidmore-Hess, Daniel, *Free Agency and Competitive Balance in Baseball*, Jefferson, NC: McFarland & Company, 2005.

James, Bill, *The New Bill James Historical Baseball Abstract*, New York, NY: Free Press, 2003.

Knight, Jonathan, *Opening Day*, Kent, OH: Kent State University Press, 2013.

Pluto, Terry, *The Curse of Rocky Colavito*, Cleveland, OH: Gray & Company, 1994.

Pluto, *Dealing: The Cleveland Indians' New Ballgame*, Cleveland, OH: Gray & Company, 2006.

Rhodes, Jean, Boburg, Shawn and Montville, Leigh, *Becoming Manny*, New York, NY: Scribner, 2009.

Schneider, Russell, *The Cleveland Indians Encyclopedia, Third Edition*, Chicago, IL: Sports Publishing, 2005.

Snyder, John, *Indians Journal*, Cincinnati, OH: Clerisy Press, 2008.

Magazines

Cleveland magazine   *Sports Illustrated*
Newsweek

Newspapers

Baltimore Sun   *Kansas City Star*
Cleveland Plain Dealer   *Los Angeles Times*
Houston Chronicle   *New York Times*

Philadelphia Daily News　　*Toledo Blade*
Seattle Times　　　　　　　*Washington Post*
Sun-Sentinel　　　　　　　 *USA Today*

Internet Sources

Baseball-Reference, baseball-reference.com
The Biz of Baseball, bizofbaseball.com
The Cleveland Memory Project, clevelandmemory.org
CNN Money, money.cnn.com
Cot's Baseball Contracts—Baseball Prospectus, baseballprospectus.com/
　　compensation/cots/
ESPN, espn.com
FanGraphs Baseball, fangraphs.com
The Hardball Times, hardballtimes.com
Major League Baseball, mlb.com
MLB.com
MLBfinances.com
Retrosheet, retrosheet.org
U.S. Census Rank by Population of the 100 Largest Urban Places,
　　census.gov/people
WeatherInsights: The Weather Channel Blog, weather.com

Wire Services

Associated Press
United Press International

Other

Cleveland Indians media guide
Cleveland Rocks: The Story of the 1995 Cleveland Indians (VHS, MLB
　　Productions, 1995)

"The Dance," released by Garth Brooks on Capitol Nashville (1990); written by Tony Arata

Korb, Donald L., Speech at Baseball Hall of Fame to Tax Section of New York State Bar Association in Cooperstown, NY (July 15, 2006).

Wahoo! What a Finish (VHS, MLB Productions, 1995)